Shabbos Workbook

The laws of Shabbos Workbook

Compiled by Rabbi Yaakov Goldstein

Shabbos Workbook

The Laws of Shabbos-Workbook
Published and copyrighted © by
Yaakov Goldstein
Rebbe Akiva 44/7 Beitar Elite, Israel
For orders, questions, comments contact:
Tel: 050-695-2866
E-mail: rabbiygoldstein@gmail.com
Available on Amazon.com
www.shulchanaruchharav.com
All rights reserved. No part of this publication may
be reproduced in any form or by any means,
Including photo-copying, without permission in
Writing from the copyright holder

5774 • 2014

Shabbos Workbook

Foreword

The workbook
The purpose of this workbook is to serve as a note taking learning aid for the corresponding Sefer of "The laws of Shabbos". The Sefer contains a lot of information with a wealth of footnotes which can be difficult to grasp and remember from mere reading. This workbook offers the learner the ability to jot his remarks and notes in each section and each Q&A discussed in the book. It is a great aid for solidifying the material and recording it to memory. It especially caters to schools, or home schools that have adopted the corresponding Sefer as part of their learning curriculum of Halacha.

Our Website:
With the help of Hashem we have established a Halacha website that caters to the Halachic needs of the law abiding G-d fearing Jew. As part of this site a special Semicha database of The laws of Shabbos has been established to help the learner research any Halacha in Semicha and have it available on his fingertips. For further information visit our site at www.shulchanaruchharav.com or email us at rabbi@shulchanaruchharav.com.

Shabbos Workbook

The laws of Shehiyah

Chapter 1: The laws of leaving a pot of food on the fire into Shabbos

1. The reason for the Shehiyah restrictions

_____

_____

2. Food that one does not plan to eat until after Shabbos

_____

_____

3. The different types of ovens and their relative laws:
A. The laws in a case when the oven is no longer Yad Soledes:

_____

_____

B. The Kirah Oven

_____

_____

C. The Tanur oven

_____

_____

D. The Kupach oven

_____

_____

E. The status of the ovens in the Alter Rebbe's times

_____

_____

F. The law when an oven is plastered shut

_____

_____

Q&A
What status of oven do our stoves and ovens have today?

_____

_____

Shabbos Workbook

<u>Additional Notes</u>

Shabbos Workbook

What status of oven do crockpots, electric plates, and water boilers have today?

How does one achieve "Ketumah" on today's stove, oven, crockpot, and electric plate?

Is there any minimum thickness that the blech must be?

May one cover the fire with tinfoil?

May one use a blech that has holes in it?

Must the entire area of the stove, electric plate, or crockpot be covered?

Must the knobs of the stove, etc. be covered?

If the blech fell off before Shabbos, must one replace it?

May one adjust the flame after having placed the blech on it?

---

4. Other forms of heat:
A. Leaving food by an open fire/Bonfire

Shabbos Workbook

Additional Notes

Shabbos Workbook

B. Leaving food on Tiberius springs from before Shabbos

_____

_____

5. Cases where the prohibition does not apply, even with a problematic oven:
A. The food is completely raw before Shabbos begins

_____

_____

B. The food has been cooked to the point of the "food of Ben Drusaiy" before Shabbos begins

_____

_____

C. What is the amount of cooking required for a dish to be considered cooked to the point of the "Machel Ben Drusaiy"?

_____

_____

Q&A on raw foods
If the raw meat will already be fully cooked before Shabbos day, does the above leniency still apply?

_____

_____

If it is possible to increase the flame and thus cause the raw meat to be fully cooked by the night meal, does the above leniency still apply?

_____

_____

When exactly before Shabbos does the raw meat have to be placed in the pot?

_____

_____

Does the leniency to place raw foods on the flame apply to any other foods other than meat?

_____

_____

Q&A on Ben Drusaiy
Is there room to require one to be stringent in accordance with the second opinion stated above, that only if the further cooking of the food is not beneficial do we allow it to be left on an open flame?

_____

_____

Shabbos Workbook

Additional Notes

Shabbos Workbook

If one accepts Shabbos early, must the food be half cooked before he accepts Shabbos, or is it enough for it to be half cooked before sunset, the time that Shabbos actually begins?

_____

_____

Does all the food in the pot need to be half cooked, or does it suffice if most of the food in the pot is half cooked?

_____

_____

How does one assess whether a food is half cooked?

_____

_____

May one on Erev Shabbos place food on an electric plate that is not yet on but will be turned on later with a timer?

_____

_____

In a pressing situation, may one be lenient and leave the food on a revealed fire if it has already cooked by one third?

_____

_____

6. The laws of Shehiyah for foods that can be eaten raw

_____

_____

7. The laws of Shehiyah for water

_____

_____

Q&A

What is the definition of half-cooked water with regard to being allowed to leave it on an uncovered flame over Shabbos?

_____

_____

Does the water or oil that is inside a heater need to be half cooked before Shabbos, if it has adjustable temperatures?

_____

_____

Shabbos Workbook

Does the water of a hot Mikveh need to be heated to its half- way point before Shabbos?

Additional Notes

Shabbos Workbook

8. What is the law if one transgressed and left a pot over a flame in a case where it was prohibited to do so?

_____

_____

Chapter 2: Placing a cooked food on an oven very close to Shabbos, without enough time for it to heat up

1. The law:

_____

_____

2. If there is enough time for the food to be heated before _Shekiah_, but not before one accepts Shabbos

_____

_____

3. Placing the pot near the oven close to Shabbos:

_____

_____

4. Placing raw meat on the fire before Shabbos according to the stringent opinion

_____

_____

Q&A

If the food is half cooked but not yet fully cooked, must it still be placed on the fire with enough time to heat up before Shabbos according to the stringent opinion?

_____

_____

Does the above stringency apply even to food being placed on a covered fire for the first time?

_____

_____

Does the above stringency apply even when placing food on an electric plate?

_____

_____

If one places the food on a high flame, does he have to leave it on the high flame until it heats up, or can he lower the flame even before it gets a chance to heat up before Shabbos?

_____

_____

Shabbos Workbook

Practical ramifications of the above stringency:

<u>Additional Notes</u>

Shabbos Workbook

Chapter 3: The laws of *Shehiyah* for roasting

1. The type of oven

_____

_____

2. Placing meat on or near the fire/coals

_____

_____

3. The law for an oven which is plastered shut

_____

_____

4. How to remove on Shabbos meat that was left roasting on top of coals or a fire

_____

_____

5. If one transgressed and left raw meat on the fire/coals from before Shabbos in a prohibited way

_____

_____

6. Placing other raw foods on or near coals right before Shabbos

_____

_____

Chapter 4: The laws of Shehiya by baking bread, and the laws of removing bread from an oven on Shabbos

1. The laws of placing bread in an oven close to Shabbos without enough time for it to fully bake:

_____

_____

2. The law if neither side of the bread had crisped before Shabbos, and it was nevertheless left in the oven

_____

_____

3. The laws of removing bread from an oven on Shabbos

_____

_____

4. The law of removing bread from an oven when it has been transgressed and the bread was placed there on Shabbos itself

_____

_____

Shabbos Workbook

Chapter 5: Preparing a bonfire before Shabbos comes in

1. Lighting wood before Shabbos

---

2. Lighting coals before Shabbos

Additional Notes

Shabbos Workbook

The laws of Chazara:

1. Placing/Returning food on a Tanur/Kupach oven, and a Kirah oven fueled with wood whose fire was not covered:

_____

_____

2. Placing/Returning food onto a Kirah oven whose coals have been covered:
A. The following 6 conditions required for one to be allowed to return a pot onto a Kirah oven on Shabbos:

_____

_____

B. The reason behind the conditions:

_____

_____

C. Placing a pot inside an oven on Shabbos

_____

_____

D. Other opinions-Those lenient to require only three conditions and to allow returning a pot to an oven

_____

_____

E. Placing the pot onto a different fire:

_____

_____

F. If the pot was insulated but not over a fire before Shabbos, may it be placed over a fire on Shabbos?

_____

_____

G. If the pot was in the oven before Shabbos may it be insulated on Shabbos?

_____

_____

Practical Q&A
Is food which is cooked to the point that further cooking will damage it allowed to be initially placed on a Kirah fire on Shabbos?

_____

_____

Shabbos Workbook

Additional Notes

Shabbos Workbook

Is an electric plate which does not have adjustable settings of heat considered to be "covered" also with regards to Chazara?

What are the laws of a crock pot with regards to having its heat covered in regards to Chazara?

If when one removed the pot there was no covering on the fire, may he now place a covering on it?

If when one removed the food from the flame, the covering [blech] fell off, may one still return it to the flame if the other conditions are fulfilled?

If the pot was removed with intention to return only after it has cooled down, may it still be returned?

If the pot fell off the fire on its own, may it be returned?

If one removed someone else's pot against their knowledge, without intention to return it, may it nevertheless be returned?

If one removed the wrong pot, without intention to return it, may it nevertheless be returned?

If ones fire extinguished, may the pots on it be transferred to a different flame?

May one place the pot down on a table if he will still leave his hand on the handle?

Shabbos Workbook

What is the law if one went ahead and placed the pot down on the counter, table, and the like?

_____

_____

What is the law if one left a pot on the stove on Erev Shabbos and then on Shabbos noticed that he did not turn on the flame, may the pot be placed on another flame?

_____

_____

If one poured the food into another pot and then placed it back into the original pot, is it permitted to return?

_____

_____

May one transfer food from one pot that is on a covered fire into another pot that is on a covered fire if all the other conditions are fulfilled?

_____

_____

How warm must it be for it to be allowed to return?

_____

_____

Is it permitted if the Chazara conditions are fulfilled to return foods into ovens which are only made to cook inside of as opposed to on top of?

_____

_____

Does a crock pot have the status of a stove or an oven in this regard?

_____

_____

Summary of the requirements needed to be allowed to add hot water to ones Chulent on Shabbos and then return it to the Crockpot:

_____

_____

If on Erev Shabbos one placed a pot on top of another pot, may he latter on Shabbos place the upper pot on the blech or electric plate?

_____

_____

Shabbos Workbook

May one move food on a Blech from one place to another place?

_____

_____

May one place a dry cooked food [as opposed to baked or roasted] near an open fire?

_____

_____

3. The Laws of placing food on top of a pot:
A. Returning food onto a fire which is covered by an empty pot:

_____

_____

B. Initially placing food on Shabbos on top of a hot pot:

_____

_____

Q&A

Does the above allowance to initially place food on a pot that is standing over a flame apply even if the pot does not have food inside it?

_____

_____

Does the food in the pot which one wants to use to place food on top of need to be fully cooked?

_____

_____

May one place the upper pot/food into the inside of the lower pot?

_____

_____

Must the upper pot/food be completely above the lower pot, or is it also ok if it sinks slightly into the lower pot?

_____

_____

May one place the pot/food over the lower pot even if the lower pot is not covered, and thus as a result of this one will be covering the lower pot?

_____

_____

If one has a double decker pot on the flame, may one place food into the upper pot?

_____

_____

Shabbos Workbook

May one place a pot on top of a pot of food that is in the oven?

<u>Additional Notes</u>

Shabbos Workbook

4. Placing food on top of a heater or any fire which is covered by a sheet of material

_____

_____

Q&A

May one initially place food directly on top of a heater/radiator?

_____

_____

May one initially place food directly onto a blech?

_____

_____

May one place Chalas on the blech in order to warm?

_____

_____

May one initially place food directly on an electric plate?

_____

_____

May one move food on a Blech from one place to another place?

_____

_____

5. Placing/returning a food near an oven:
A. Placing food next to the wall of a Kirah oven on Shabbos:

_____

_____

B. Placing food next to a stove top/open fire?

_____

_____

C. Placing food next to a Tanur and Kupach oven:

_____

_____

6. Placing food on Shabbos by an area which is not Yad Soledes Bo:
A. Placing it near the oven by an area which is not Yad Soledes:

_____

_____

Shabbos Workbook

Additional Notes

Shabbos Workbook

B. Placing it on an oven by an area which is not Yad Soledes

_____

_____

C. Returning food into an oven on Shabbos that is not Yad Soledes:

_____

_____

7. Placing food on a heater which will eventually turn on:
A. Having a Jew place it:

_____

_____

B. Telling a gentile to place food by a heater which will only turn on at a later time:

_____

_____

Q&A
May one on Erev Shabbos place food on his electric plate which is not yet on but will turn on latter with the timer?

_____

_____

May one on Shabbos itself initially place food on his electric plate which is not yet on but will turn on latter with the timer?

_____

_____

May one place food into an oven which will eventually turn on?

_____

_____

8. If one transgressed the above conditions
A. The law if one placed a food on a flame on Shabbos without fulfilling the required conditions:

_____

_____

B. If a gentile placed ones food onto an oven on Shabbos, in a way prohibited for a Jew to do, is the food permitted?

_____

_____

Shabbos Workbook

Additional Notes

Shabbos Workbook

The laws of Hatmanah:

Chapter 1: Insulating food on Erev Shabbos-Insulation which increases heat

1. The Mitzvah to insulate food on Erev Shabbos.

_____

_____

Q&A
Must one specifically insulate his food, or is it ok also if he leaves it on the fire from Erev Shabbos?

_____

_____

2. The prohibition to insulate with materials that increase heat:
A. The prohibition, its reasoning and if it applies by cooked food

_____

_____

B. Insulating completely raw meat right before Shabbos begins:

_____

_____

C. Insulating foods before Shabbos which one does not plan to eat until Shabbos day

_____

_____

3. The definition of insulation:
A. The law if the insulation does not touch the walls of the pot:

_____

_____

B. How much of the pot must be insulated for it to be considered a prohibited insulation?

_____

_____

Q&A
If one insulates around a pot that has handles, and thus by the area of the handles the material is not touching the pot, is this still considered insulation?

_____

_____

Shabbos Workbook

Additional Notes

Shabbos Workbook

According to the Alter Rebbe's ruling in the Mahadurha Basra that even insulating the top of a vessel is problematic, would it be prohibited on Shabbos to place a wide pot on top of a pot of hot food and then cover it with a towel, being that the wide pot touches the cover of the pot?

_____

_____

If the food does not fill the entire pot, is it still considered insulated if the majority area of the walls where the food reaches to is insulated?

_____

_____

4. Which materials are considered to add heat?

_____

_____

Q&A

What is the status of blankets and pillows?

_____

_____

What is the status of a crock pot?

_____

_____

May one insulate on Shabbos with materials that do not add heat and are never commonly used to insulate with?

_____

_____

5. Insulating within the Tiberius hot springs
A. Placing a bottle of water and the like into the spring from before Shabbos:

_____

_____

B. Having cold water flow into the hot spring from before Shabbos:

_____

_____

6. Insulating before Shabbos with non-heat adding material however on top of material that adds heat, such as a blech

_____

_____

Shabbos Workbook

Additional Notes

Shabbos Workbook

Q&A

May one on Erev Shabbos place an insulated pot onto a blech or an electric plate

_____

_____

May one on Erev Shabbos enter food that is inside a small pot into a pot of food that is on the fire, such as to place a small kugel that is in a pot inside ones Chulent?

_____

_____

May one on Erev Shabbos enter food that is wrapped with tin foil or plastic wrap into a pot of food that is on the fire, such as to place wrapped Kishkeh onto ones Chulent?

_____

_____

May one place a pot insulated with material that does not add heat inside of an oven that has been turned off, or an electric plate that is now off?

_____

_____

May one place on Shabbos food which is wrapped in tinfoil on top of a pot that is on a flame?

_____

_____

May one on Erev Shabbos place food wrapped in tinfoil onto his blech or electric plate?

_____

_____

May one on Shabbos place a pot cover over food that is resting on top of another pot that is on the fire?

_____

_____

May one on Erev Shabbos insulate food inside a hot pot of water that is off the fire?

_____

_____

May this be done even if the pot is on a flame or blech or electric plate?

_____

_____

7. Placing a non-insulated pot of food directly on top of coals of an oven or any fire:

_____

_____

Shabbos Workbook

Additional Notes

Shabbos Workbook

Q&A

According to the Beis Yosef [Sefaradim] may one leave food on a blech or electric plate on Erev Shabbos if it is completely not insulated?

_____

_____

Should one be stringent like the 1ˢᵗ opinion to Lechatchilah not place a pot directly on coals

_____

_____

8. The laws of Hatmanah in a case that the oven has been sealed shut with plaster:

_____

_____

9. The law if one transgressed and insulated in material which adds heat:

_____

_____

Q&A

If one went ahead and insulated food which has been cooked to the point of Ben Drusaiy, may he be lenient like the opinions that permit this, and thus be allowed to eat it on Shabbos?

_____

_____

If one transgressed and insulated food with a heating material is the food permitted immediately after Shabbos, or does one need to wait until enough time passes for it to heat up?

_____

_____

Chapter 2: Insulating food on Shabbos-Insulation which does not add heat

1. Insulating food on Shabbos itself

_____

_____

2. The definition of insulation :
A. The law if the insulation does not touch the walls of the pot:

_____

_____

B. How much of the pot must be insulated for it to be considered a prohibited insulation?

_____

_____

Shabbos Workbook

Additional Notes

Shabbos Workbook

Q&A
How much of the pot must be insulated for it to be considered a prohibited insulation?

_____

_____

3. Is it permitted to insulate by Bein Hashmashos on Erev Shabbos?

_____

_____

Q&A
If one had accepted Shabbos early, may he still insulate with material that does not add heat until after Bein Hashmashos?

_____

_____

May one who lit candles do Hatmanah until Bein Hashmashos?

_____

_____

4. What is the law if one insulated food on Shabbos?

_____

_____

5. Scenarios in which insulating on Shabbos is permitted:
A. Placing an upside down pot over a hot pot on Shabbos:

_____

_____

B. Covering the pot in order to guard it:

_____

_____

C. May one re-insulate on Shabbos a pot that had been insulated before Shabbos?

_____

_____

D. Insulating on Shabbos food which has been transferred to a different pot.

_____

_____

E. Insulating cold food on Shabbos:

_____

_____

Shabbos Workbook

Q&A

May one reinsulate a pot that was insulated before Shabbos even if he removed the pot from the insulation, or only if he removed the insulation from the pot, leaving the pot in its original area?

_____

_____

May one re-insulate a pot or add insulation to a pot that was insulated before Shabbos even if the food is not fully cooked?

_____

_____

Does this permission apply even if the food is a solid substance ["Davar Gush"]?

_____

_____

May one place hot water on Shabbos into an insulation thermos?

_____

_____

May one on Shabbos place a cold bottle or other food into a hot pot of water that is off the fire?

_____

_____

Additional Notes

Shabbos Workbook

The laws of cooking
Chapter 1: The cooking prohibition

1. The Biblically forbidden forms of cooking:

A. The Principal prohibition:

_____

_____

B. The forms of cooking

_____

_____

C. The forms of heating

_____

_____

D. The forms of foods and the heating level defined as cooking:

_____

_____

Q&A

Does the prohibition to soften or harden a non-food item apply even if he does not have intent to do so and it inevitably occurs?

_____

_____

May one pour boiling water into a plastic cup if it will cause it to melt?

_____

_____

Is melting/softening an object forbidden even to less than Yad Soledes?

_____

_____

Is the prohibition to soften an object applicable also by food, such as to place bread or Matzah in soup and the like?

_____

_____

May one toast bread near a fire on Shabbos or is this considered forbidden due to hardening a soft object?

_____

_____

Shabbos Workbook

Additional Notes

Shabbos Workbook

May one heat an egg on Shabbos to the point it becomes hard boiled?

_____

_____

2. The Rabbinically forbidden forms of cooking:

_____

_____

Q&A

What form of cooking is considered electric heat?

_____

_____

3. The permitted forms of cooking/heating

_____

_____

Q&A

May one use a magnifying glass to cook his food?

_____

_____

4. Heating uncooked foods and liquids on Shabbos to less than Yad Soledes Bo:
A. Placing cold liquids on top of a kettle:

_____

_____

B. Placing hot uncooked food on top of a hot pot so it retain is heat:

_____

_____

C. Sealing the cover of a pot of uncooked food on Shabbos:

_____

_____

D. Placing uncooked foods near a fire on Shabbos:

_____

_____

Shabbos Workbook

Q&A
A food which will be damaged if warmed to Yad Soledes may it be warmed near a fire where it can reach Yad Soledes due to that one will not come to forget to remove it prior to it reaching that point?

<u>Additional Notes</u>

Shabbos Workbook

May one place a baby bottle with substance that has a cooking prohibition into a Keli Rishon or near a fire with intent to remove it prior to it reaching Yad Soledes?

_____

_____

May one melt a frozen baby bottle in the sun or near heat in an area that it will not reach Yad Soledes?

_____

_____

May one warm or dry his wet hands near a heater or fire?

_____

_____

5. Stirring a pot of hot food and removing its content
A. Not fully cooked-May not remove the food while hot:

_____

_____

B. Fully cooked:

_____

_____

Q&A On Uncooked Foods:
What should one do if he already removed the food from the fire but then realized that it is not yet fully cooked?

_____

_____

May one remove uncooked food from a hot Keli Sheiyni?

_____

_____

May one remove the uncooked food with a fork?

_____

_____

If some of the food in the pot is fully cooked, may the fully cooked foods be removed from the pot?

_____

_____

May one stir uncooked food that is in a Keli Sheiyni?

_____

_____

Shabbos Workbook

<u>Additional Notes</u>

Shabbos Workbook

Q&A on Cooked food that is on the fire

May one stir cooked Yad Soledes water that is on the fire?

_____

_____

May one stir on the fire a food which has no liquid, such as a piece of Kugel?

_____

_____

If the pot has been moved off the fire but is still on the blech may it be mixed or have food taken out from it?

_____

_____

May one pour water of a Keli Rishon onto a pot of cooked food that is on the fire?

_____

_____

May one remove water from a pot of water that is on the fire?

_____

_____

If the pot of fully cooked food is too heavy to remove from the fire how is one to remove food from it?

_____

_____

May one pour water of a Keli Rishon onto a pot of cooked food that is off the fire?

_____

_____

When allowed to remove food may one remove food from even the bottom of the pot?

_____

_____

6. Heating liquid that was previously cooked to the point of Yad Soledes:

_____

_____

Q&A

When is a liquid considered pre-cooked?

_____

_____

Shabbos Workbook

__Additional Notes__

Shabbos Workbook

If a liquid had been originally cooked to only Yad Soledes and is still warm may it be heated even past Yad Soledes, to boiling point?

Should one ideally be stringent like the Michaber's opinion which holds that so long as the liquid is below Yad Soledes it is forbidden to reheat due to cooking?

If the precooked liquid which has fully cooled down had cooked to the point of "condensing in a way damaging for the owner" is it still forbidden to reheat?

Is fruit juice considered a liquid?

Are pure jam or paste, and the like of other pure fruit /vegetable pastes, considered like a liquid or solid?

Is ketchup considered a liquid?

May one reheat a doughnut with jam inside?

If the liquid fully cooled down, and then got reheated, such as by placing it into a Keli Sheiyni, which is allowed, then may one place it into a Keli Rishon?

May one use a wet spoon or ladle to remove soup from a pot that is off the fire?

7. Heating a dry solid which was previously cooked, or roasted, or baked to the point of Yad Soledes:

Shabbos Workbook

<u>Additional Notes</u>

Shabbos Workbook

Q&A

What is the definition of a dry solid?

_____

_____

Do chicken bones need to be cooked to be allowed to further heat the chicken or dish that they are in?

_____

_____

What foods are considered cooked as opposed to baked or roasted?

_____

_____

Is placing a food defined as cooked into an empty pot near the fire considered roasting?

_____

_____

May one place a food defined as cooked on top of a pot that is on the fire?

_____

_____

May one place soup nuggets into soup that is a Keli Rishon or Sheiyni?

_____

_____

May one place bread into soup that is a Keli Rishon/Sheiyni?

_____

_____

May one place a food defined as roasted or baked into an empty pot near the fire?

_____

_____

May one place bread on top of a hot cooked potato or hot piece of cooked meat?

_____

_____

May one place dry Yerushalmi Kugel into a Keli Sheiyni bowl of hot chulent and the like?

_____

_____

Shabbos Workbook

<u>Additional Notes</u>

Shabbos Workbook

May one heat near a fire water that is still warm which was cooked using sun heat?

_____

_____

May food cooked through a microwave be later heated through heat of a fire?

_____

_____

May one heat on Shabbos to Yad Soledes a raw food which was salted or pickled?

_____

_____

May one move a pot of fully cooked food which is on the blech closer to the flame in order so its liquid condenses?

_____

_____

8. Heating precooked/baked foods on Shabbos which dissolve/melt in heat [such as congealed fat and oil]:
A. The Ruling of Admur in the Shulchan Aruch regarding the cooking prohibition:

_____

_____

B. The First Opinion In the Shulchan Aruch regarding the Nolad prohibition:

_____

_____

C. The Second Opinion in the Shulchan Aruch:

_____

_____

D. The Final Ruling In Shulchan Aruch:

_____

_____

E. The ruling of the Siddur regarding the cooking prohibition, which is the Final Ruling of Today:

_____

_____

Q&A

What is the definition of a dry solid?

_____

_____

Shabbos Workbook

Additional Notes

Shabbos Workbook

List of items which dissolve and thus have a cooking prohibition even if they were previously cooked:

Food which is dry but upon being heated it releases gravy or oil, is it forbidden to heat on Shabbos?

9. The laws of a Keli Rishon
A. Precooked/prebaked foods:

B. Uncooked foods:

C. If one transgressed and placed spices into a Keli Rishon:

D. If the Keli Rishon is no longer Yad Soledes:

E. Pouring water into a Keli Rishon

F. Placing cold water into an empty Keli Rishon

Q&A

Must one pour or the cold water into the Keli Rishon in one splash, or may one pour it in continuously until enough water enters for the Keli Rishon to be under Yad Soledes?

May one place a bottle of liquid in a Keli Rishon that is no longer Yad Soledes in order to thaw it down?

Shabbos Workbook

Additional Notes

Shabbos Workbook

General Q&A

May one remove the pot from the stove using a damp cloth or mitten?

_____

_____

Must the spoon used to remove food from a Keli Rishon be dry?

_____

_____

When replacing a cover onto a Keli Rishon must one make sure that the inner side of the cover is dry from the perspiration that it received during cooking?

_____

_____

Q&A on definition of a Keli Rishon

Is a boiler which has heating coils inside of its vessel, such as some Kumkums, are they considered like a Keli Rishon?

_____

_____

Is water poured from a Keli Rishon while still on the fire into a vessel considered a Keli Rishon, such as a water boiler which has a spout with which to pour out the water?

_____

_____

If one poured the food of a Keli Rishon into another pot which it itself is hot due to having been heated over a fire, does that food still have the status of a Keli Rishon?

_____

_____

What is the law of a food which is removed with a ladle from a Keli Rishon?

_____

_____

If one poured food from a Keli Sheiyni back into a hot Keli Rishon does it still retain the status of a Keli Sheiyni?

_____

_____

Q&A

On opening and closing the hot water of sinks and the like:

_____

_____

Shabbos Workbook

Additional Notes

Shabbos Workbook

May one open the hot water tab if by doing so cold water will be caused to enter into the boiler?

May one in such a case ask a gentile to open up the hot water tab, such as in order to warm a cold Mikveh?

May one open the hot water if one knows for certain that the water in the boiler is no longer Yad Soledes?

May one open the hot water if he closed the pipes thus not allowing any cold water to enter into the boiler?

May one initially leave open from Erev Shabbos the hot faucet?

May one further open the faucet on Shabbos when left open before Shabbos?

May one close a faucet of hot water that was left open before Shabbos or was accidentally opened on Shabbos?

May one ask a gentile to close the hot water faucet that was left open?

When left open may one open the cold water?

---

10. Very hot water of a Keli Sheiyni has the same status as a Keli Rishon

---

Shabbos Workbook

<u>**Additional Notes**</u>

Shabbos Workbook

Q&A on a very hot Keli Sheyni:

What is the definition of a very hot Keli Sheyni which has the status of a Keli Rishon?

_____

_____

Is the prohibition to pour cold liquids into a very hot Keli Sheiyni only with regards to water or is it also with regards to other liquids such as milk?

_____

_____

May one pour from a very hot Keli Sheiyni onto a food?

_____

_____

What is the law of a very hot Keli Shelishi?

_____

_____

May one pour cold water into a very hot Mikveh?

_____

_____

May one remove the plug of a Mikveh which attaches it to the rainwater?

_____

_____

Must one who enters into a very hot Mikvah on Shabbos verify that his feet are dry prior to entering?

_____

_____

Does a thermos have the status of a Keli Rishon or Sheiyni?

_____

_____

11. A Davar Gush/Placing a solid substance onto a food or liquid and Vice versa:

_____

_____

Q&A on a Davar Gush:

What is the definition of a Davar Gush/ Solid food?

_____

_____

Shabbos Workbook

Additional Notes

Shabbos Workbook

Is a Davar Gush always considered a Keli Rishon even when placed into another vessel?

_____

_____

When a Davar Gush is picked up with a fork from a Keli Rishon does it now have the status of a Keli Sheiyni according to the lenient opinion?

_____

_____

If a Davar Gush was placed into soup that is in a second dish, does it receive a Keli Sheiyni status according to all?

_____

_____

May one place ketchup onto a Yad Soledes Davar Gush which was placed on a Keli Shelishi according to the stringent opinion?

_____

_____

May one place butter or margarine on a Yad Soledes Davar Gush that has been placed in a Keli Shelishi according to the stringent opinion?

_____

_____

Is a solid piece of food that is placed together with liquid into a second vessel still considered a Keli Rishon [according to the stringent opinions], such as for example, soup that has solid pieces which are poured into a bowl?

_____

_____

12. Iruiy Keli Rishon/Pouring from a Keli Rishon onto uncooked food

_____

_____

Q&A

May one pour from a Keli Rishon onto the outside walls of a vessel which contains in it food?

_____

_____

If the stream being poured from the Keli Rishon is not attached to its source by the time it hits the food is it still considered like the pouring of a Keli Rishon?

_____

_____

Shabbos Workbook

Additional Notes

Shabbos Workbook

Is hot water which comes from the sink considered the pouring of a Keli Rishon?

_____

_____

If one pours from a Keli Rishon onto the inner walls of a pot of food, having it flow from the wall of the pot onto the food, does that water still have the status of the pouring of a Keli Rishon?

_____

_____

May one pour from a Keli Rishon onto a food which had already been poured on from a Keli Rishon from before Shabbos?

_____

_____

If the food being poured on was previously soaked in a Keli Rishon is it then allowed?

_____

_____

Q&A on pouring liquid/food from a Keli Rishon onto cold water
Must one dry his cup prior to pouring water from a Keli Rishon onto it?

_____

_____

May one pour from a Keli Rishon onto water even if the Keli Rishon is still on the fire?

_____

_____

May one pour from a Keli Rishon onto fat?

_____

_____

May one pour hot water onto a plate which has fat smeared on it, such as to rinse it off?

_____

_____

May one place a Davar Gush Keli Rishon into a large amount of water?

_____

_____

May one place a Keli Rishon Davar gush on a slightly wet plate?

_____

_____

Shabbos Workbook

Additional Notes

Shabbos Workbook

May one place a hot egg from a Keli Rishon into a cup of water to cool it down?

_____

_____

May one place a Keli Rishon vessel/pot in cold water in order to cool off the vessel/pot?

_____

_____

May one place a Keli Rishon pot onto a wet surface/counter/towel?

_____

_____

May one place a hot pot which has been emptied of its food into a sink filled with water?

_____

_____

May one pour cold water into a hot Keli Rishon pot which has been emptied of its food?

_____

_____

May one remove a pot from the fire using a wet towel?

_____

_____

May one rinse off a hot Keli Rishon egg under a faucet of cold water?

_____

_____

May one rinse a hot piece of meat under a faucet of cold water?

_____

_____

13. The Laws of a Keli Sheiyni

_____

_____

Q&A

What is the definition of a spice?

_____

_____

Shabbos Workbook

Additional Notes

Shabbos Workbook

Are spices which were not around in the times of the Sages considered spices regarding the leniency to place them in a Keli Sheiyni?

_____

_____

Are spices which are questionable whether they were used as spices in the times of the Sages considered spices regarding the leniency to place them in a Keli Sheiyni?

_____

_____

May one place substances which dissolve and become liquid into a Keli Sheiyni?

_____

_____

A list of foods which are and are not considered spices:

_____

_____

Are precooked liquids which have cooled off allowed to be placed in a Keli Sheiyni?

_____

_____

May one place a very small amount of cold water into a large amount of hot water that is in a Keli Sheiyni?

_____

_____

When using a spoon/ladle to remove food from a Keli Sheiyni must that spoon be dry?

_____

_____

Is placing spices and liquids in a Keli Sheiyni allowed even if they will become Yad Soledes?

_____

_____

If a food had soaked in a Keli Rishon before Shabbos may it be placed in a Keli Sheiyni on Shabbos?

_____

_____

If food was poured on from a Keli Rishon or soaked in a Keli Sheiyni before Shabbos may it be placed in a Keli Sheiyni on Shabbos?

_____

_____

Shabbos Workbook

Additional Notes

Shabbos Workbook

What is the law of a food which is removed with a ladle from a Keli Sheiyni?

_____

_____

May one place a Keli Sheiyni vessel into cold water in order to cool it down?

_____

_____

May one place honey into a Keli Sheiyni?

_____

_____

14. Iruiy Keli Sheiyni [pouring from a Keli Sheiyni onto uncooked foods:

_____

_____

Q&A

If the Keli Sheiyni is no longer Yad Soledes may it be poured onto the light foods?

_____

_____

May one pour from a Yad Soledes Keli Sheiyni onto herring?

_____

_____

Are foods other than those listed above which one sees that they cook with the pouring of a Keli Sheiny also forbidden to be poured on?

_____

_____

Examples of lightly cooked foods:

_____

_____

If one poured from a Keli Sheiyni on to the light foods before Shabbos may he redo this on Shabbos?

_____

_____

May one pour from a Keli Sheiyni onto foods which will dissolve?

_____

_____

Shabbos Workbook

Additional Notes

Shabbos Workbook

A Keli Shelishi:

_____

_____

May one place tea in a Keli Shelishi?

_____

15. Opening the oven on Shabbos when there are still burning coals inside of it?

_____

Q&A

May one open an oven on Shabbos which is on and works based on thermostat?

_____

_____

16. Issur which fell into one's food on Shabbos:

_____

General Q&A

A. Covering a pot of food that is on the fire or that is not fully cooked:

May one return a cover back onto a pot of food that is on the fire?

_____

May one return a cover back onto a pot of none fully cooked food that is off the fire?

_____

May one place a cloth or the like on a pot that is on the fire to insulate it in a way that does not pose a Hatmanah prohibition?

_____

May one place a cloth or the like on a pot of non-fully cooked food that is off the fire?

_____

May one move a pot of food that is on the blech to a hotter spot?

_____

Shabbos Workbook

Additional Notes

Shabbos Workbook

B. Q&A which relate to electrical heating systems:

May an electric water urn be used for Shabbos?

_____

_____

May one on Erev Shabbos place food on his electric plate which is not yet on but will turn on latter with the timer?

_____

_____

May one on Shabbos itself initially place food on his electric plate which is not yet on but will turn on latter with the timer?

_____

_____

May one adjust the timer of the Shabbos clock on Shabbos?

_____

_____

May one adjust the temperature of a heater?

_____

_____

May one adjust the temperature of an air conditioner?

_____

_____

May one open or close the windows of his house if this will cause the air conditioner or heater to turn on or turn off quicker?

_____

_____

May one open the door of his fridge if it will cause the motor to turn on or last longer?

_____

_____

Summary of preparing coffee, tea, soup mix, baby formula on Shabbos:

_____

_____

Shabbos Workbook

<u>Additional Notes</u>

Shabbos Workbook

Chapter 2: The law of food of which one transgressed a prohibition with on Shabbos

1. The intentional transgressor:

2. The Unintentional transgressor:

3. The law if one transgressed and cooked a food of which there are opinions which permit it to be done even initially:

4. What is the law if the forbidden food got mixed into other foods?

5. Is food that had a transgression done to it on behalf of an ill person allowed to be eaten by others?

6. Fruits that were cut down on Shabbos on behalf of a sick person:

7. What is the law if one transgressed and left a pot over a flame in a case that it was prohibited to do so?

8. The law if one placed a food on a flame on Shabbos without fulfilling the required conditions?

9. If a gentile placed ones food onto an oven on Shabbos, in a way prohibited for a Jew to do, is the food permitted?

10. The law if one transgressed and insulated in material which adds heat

Shabbos Workbook

Additional Notes

Shabbos Workbook

Q&A

If one went ahead and insulated food which has been cooked to the point of Ben Drusaiy, may he be lenient like the opinions that permit this, and thus be allowed to eat it on Shabbos?

If one transgressed and insulated food with a heating material is the food permitted immediately after Shabbos, or does one need to wait until enough time passes for it to heat up?

What is the law if one intentionally transgressed a Rabbinical prohibition on Shabbos?

What is the law if one unintentionally transgressed a Rabbinical prohibition on Shabbos?

Does this rule apply to all prohibitions which are disputed, such as cooking a food which was already cooked to the point of Ben Drusaiy?

Shabbos Workbook

<u>**Additional Notes**</u>

Shabbos Workbook

The laws of Muktzah
Chapter 1: The General laws of Muktzah

1. The reasons behind the Muktzah prohibition:

2. When was the Muktzah prohibition instituted?

3. The General Rules Of Muktzah:
A. May one move a Muktzah item using parts of his body other than his hands?

Q&A
May one move a Muktzah item using an irregularity for no reason at all?

Is carrying an item with one hand, if it usually requires two hands, an irregularity?

Is carrying an item with two people, if usually it can be carried alone, considered an irregularity?

Is carrying an item using two fingers considered an irregularity?

B. Using a non-Muktzah item to move Muktzah:

C. May one touch a Muktzah item?

Shabbos Workbook

<u>Additional Notes</u>

Shabbos Workbook

D. Removing an item from on top of a Muktzah item:

_____

_____

E. May one place an item on top of something Muktzah?

_____

_____

F. Bittul Keli Meheichano: May one place a non-Muktzah item under a Muktzah item, to catch it just in case it falls?

_____

_____

G. May one sit on a Muktzah item:

_____

_____

Q&A

May one sit on a car?

_____

_____

May one open the door of a car and sit inside it?

_____

_____

H. Getting benefit from Muktzah:

_____

_____

I. What does one do if he accidently picked up a Muktzah object or realized that he was carrying Muktzah?

_____

_____

Q&A

If one remembered that he is carrying a Muktzah item in his pocket or on his belt and dropping it does not involve loss, may he nevertheless bring it to a desired area?

_____

_____

May one switch hands when holding a Muktzah object which one mistakenly picked up?

_____

_____

Shabbos Workbook

<u>Additional Notes</u>

Shabbos Workbook

J. Moving Muktzah through a gentile:

_____

_____

K. May one move Muktzah items if they are a safety hazard?

_____

_____

Q&A

If an item poses a safety hazard only to an individual, such as he is the only one home, may it be moved?

_____

_____

How many people are defined as a public for it to be considered a public safety hazard?

_____

_____

If the people are able to avoid the hazard may it nevertheless be moved?

_____

_____

May a pit in a public area be covered?

_____

_____

May one turn off the gas of a stove of which its fire extinguished?

_____

_____

L. The law of Muktzah items which are repulsive

_____

_____

Q&A

May one move a clean potty?

_____

_____

M. The law of Muktzah items which underwent a change on Shabbos and lost their reason to be Muktzah:

_____

_____

Shabbos Workbook

<u>Additional Notes</u>

Shabbos Workbook

Q&A

Are non-edibles due to lack of being cooked considered MM"G when belonging to a non-Jew?

_____

_____

Are raw foods which one began cooking right before Shabbos in a permitted way considered Muktzah until they are ready?

_____

_____

The categories of Muktzah and their corresponding laws

4. Muktzah Machmas Chisaron Kis-Items of value which are not used for other than their set purpose:

A. Its definition:

_____

_____

B. The law of items defined as MMC"K:

_____

_____

C. If one decided before Shabbos to use the item on Shabbos:

_____

_____

D. Examples of items which have the status of Muktzah Machamas Chisaron Kis:

_____

_____

E. What is the status of the pieces of a MMC"K vessel that shattered on Shabbos?

_____

_____

Q&A on Merchandise

Is Merchandise with which one is not particular against using considered a Keli Shemilachto Leisur?

_____

_____

Is an inexpensive item which one is particular against using for matters other than its intent, considered Muktzah Machmas Chisaron Kis?

_____

_____

Shabbos Workbook

Additional Notes

Shabbos Workbook

Is blank paper today considered Muktzah?

Are expensive decorations or items of sentimental value, which people avoid using for any purpose considered MMC"K? Examples- Are clocks, and pictures which are set on the wall Muktzah?

Are closets and book cases which are designated to a specific area Muktzah?

Does Ch"k go according to each person's personal assessment on the item or is it in accordance to ones general society treats it?

Is Matzah considered Muktzah on Shabbos that falls on Erev Pesach?

According to the Chabad custom to avoid Matzah 30 days before Pesach would the Matzah Mitzvah be Muktzah on all the Shabbosim that fall 30 days before Pesach?

Is a Pasul Sefer Torah Muktzah?

Are candlesticks considered Muktzah?

Are Sefarim which are designated to be sold, such as at a book store, or old manuscripts, considered Muktzah?

Is a manuscript of words of Torah meant for editing considered Muktzah?

Shabbos Workbook

Additional Notes

Shabbos Workbook

Are clothing and other merchandise which are designated to be sold considered Muktzah?

_____

_____

Is an esrog Muktzah?

_____

_____

5. Muktzah Machmas Issur-Items designated for forbidden use:
A. Its definition

_____

_____

B. Its law regarding what purposes it may be moved for?

_____

_____

C. Does placing a baby or bread on a Muktzah item remove its moving restrictions?

_____

_____

D. If a MM"I item has been picked up for its space does it need to be placed down right away?

_____

_____

E. Moving a MM"I item for the sake of another person:

_____

_____

F. Examples of items which may be considered MM"I:
Food utensils which have food in them:

_____

_____

Musical instruments:

_____

_____

Is a broom Muktzah?

_____

_____

Shabbos Workbook

Additional Notes

Shabbos Workbook

Under what status of Muktzah do Tefillin fall under?

_____

_____

Q&A

May one remove Tefillin from his bedroom in order to be permitted to have marital relations?

_____

_____

May one remove his Tallis from his Tefillin bag on Shabbos?

_____

_____

May one move the large bag in which one usually places his Tallis and Tefillin inside of, although on Shabbos only his Tefillin are left inside of it?

_____

_____

May one move his Tefillin out from the rain or from the sun?

_____

_____

Is a needle Muktzah?

_____

_____

May one enter shoetrees into his shoes on Shabbos to upkeep the shoes?

_____

_____

Is a clock Muktzah?

_____

_____

G. Moving candles, candle sticks, lamps and candelabras on Shabbos:

_____

_____

Are today's candlesticks considered Muktzah?

_____

_____

Shabbos Workbook

<u>Additional Notes</u>

Shabbos Workbook

H. Wet laundry:

_____

_____

Are clothing which were wet by Bein Hashmashos considered Muktzah?

_____

_____

I. Books and other writings which are forbidden to be read on Shabbos:

_____

_____

Q&A

Are newspapers which are forbidden to be read Muktzah?

_____

_____

If Muktzah writings were intentionally placed on a Sefer does that Sefer become Muktzah?

_____

_____

General Q&A

What is defined as moving an object for use of its space (limikomo)?

_____

_____

What is defined as moving an object for use of itself (Ligufo)?

_____

_____

May one move a MM"I object for a permissible use if one is also able to do the task with a non-Muktzah object?

_____

_____

May one switch hands when holding a MM"I object which one picked up in order to use its place?

_____

_____

When holding a MM"I object which one picked up in order to use its space may one continue walking with it if he stopped but did not yet put it down?

_____

_____

Shabbos Workbook

Additional Notes

Shabbos Workbook

May one move a MM"I object in order to prevent it from damaging non-Muktzah items?

_____

_____

May one move a MM"I object in order to prevent it from damaging Muktzah items?

_____

_____

May one move a MM"I object to prevent it from being damaged if he plans to use it that Shabbos?

_____

_____

Is a lamp considered MM"I?

_____

_____

Is a fan Muktzah?

_____

_____

Are car keys Muktzah?

_____

_____

Is a Megilah Muktzah on Shabbos?

_____

_____

Is a Mezuzah MM"I?

_____

_____

6. Muktzah Machamas Gufo-Items which do not have the status of a vessel:
A. The definition and law

_____

_____

B. Foods which are defined as MM"G:

_____

_____

Shabbos Workbook

<u>Additional Notes</u>

Shabbos Workbook

C. Items which are defined as MM"G and how they can be designated to become a vessel:
May one play ball on Shabbos?

———————————————————————————————

———————————————————————————————

Are Shatnez clothing Muktzah?

———————————————————————————————

———————————————————————————————

Is rainwater considered Muktzah?

———————————————————————————————

———————————————————————————————

D. What is the status of an item that was turned into a vessel on Shabbos by a gentile?

———————————————————————————————

———————————————————————————————

E. Moving Animals

———————————————————————————————

———————————————————————————————

Q&A

Are non-edibles due to lack of being cooked considered MM"G when belonging to a non-Jew?

———————————————————————————————

———————————————————————————————

Are raw foods Muktzah on Yom Tov?

———————————————————————————————

———————————————————————————————

Is food with a Hechsher that one does not rely upon considered Muktzah?

———————————————————————————————

———————————————————————————————

Is Gebrocks/Matzah Shruya Muktzah for one who is stringent not to eat it?

———————————————————————————————

———————————————————————————————

Is Kitniyos Muktzah for Ashkenazim on Pesach?

———————————————————————————————

———————————————————————————————

Shabbos Workbook

Additional Notes

Shabbos Workbook

May one move an aquarium or bird cage on Shabbos ?

Does a frozen food which can only be eaten when it defrosts considered Muktzah?

If ones freezer has lost electricity, may the raw meets be moved to another freezer?

Are foods which are in the midst of pickling process considered Muktzah?

Are raw foods which one began cooking right before Shabbos in a permitted way considered Muktzah until they are ready?

May one play with play dough on Shabbos?

If a certain inedible food is edible for a commonly found animal, but due to lack of an Eiruv one is not able to feed the animal that food on Shabbos, does the food become Muktzah?

May one play ball on Shabbos?

May one play ping pong on Shabbos?

May one remove the drain cover of one's floor on Shabbos?

Shabbos Workbook

Additional Notes

Shabbos Workbook

7. Keli Shemilachto Liheter-The laws of vessels designated for permitted use:
A. Definition and law:-May move even to save from damage:

_____

_____

B. The law regarding moving food and Torah books:

_____

_____

C. Moving an object for a non-immediate use:

_____

_____

D. Items that are considered Keli Shemilachto Liheter:

_____

_____

Q&A

May one twiddle a non-Muktzah item in his hand for mere enjoyment?

_____

_____

What is the law of an item which contains a Muktzah part and a Non-Muktzah part which are inseparable?

_____

_____

8. Keli SheMuktzah Machmas Miuso/A vessel which is avoided due to its repulsiveness:

_____

_____

9. Muktzah Machmas Mitzvah:
A. May one use a Yom Tov candle for other purposes?

_____

_____

B. The Schach, walls and ornaments of a Sukkah:

_____

_____

10. Summary of the Muktzah categories:

_____

_____

Shabbos Workbook

Additional Notes

Shabbos Workbook

11. The laws of vessels which have broken on Shabbos:
A. What is the status of the pieces of a non-Muktzah vessel that shattered on Shabbos?

_____

_____

-If the broken pieces are still fit for their original purpose:

_____

_____

-If the broken pieces are no longer fit for any use

_____

_____

B. What is the status of the pieces of a Muktzah vessel that shattered on Shabbos?

_____

_____

C. If the pieces of the broken vessel were thrown out:

_____

_____

D. May one move Muktzah items if they are a safety hazard?

_____

_____

E. Vessels which have disassembled on Shabbos:

_____

_____

F. Examples of broken vessels:
The status of a broken wick:

_____

_____

Is a broken sandal Muktzah?

_____

_____

A needle which has lost its head or its hole:

_____

_____

Shabbos Workbook

Additional Notes

Shabbos Workbook

G. Worn out cloths:

_____

_____

H. May one break a piece off a broken vessel in order to use for a purpose on Shabbos?

_____

_____

Q&A

When do pieces broken from a vessel retain their non-Muktzah, vessel, status?

_____

_____

If a MM"I object broke on Shabbos do the pieces remain MM"I even if they have a use (such as a covering)?

_____

_____

When do we make a decree of Muktzah on items that have broken and can be re-fixed after Shabbos?

_____

_____

What degree of Muktzah do items that have broken, and we suspect will be fixed on Shabbos, receive?

_____

_____

How is one permitted to move an attached door on Shabbos if it is considered a non-vessel?

_____

_____

Is a detached door of a MMC"K vessel considered Muktzah?

_____

_____

Are buttons Muktzah:

_____

_____

Is Sheimos which is in a bin Muktzah?

_____

_____

Shabbos Workbook

Additional Notes

Shabbos Workbook

May one fix broken glasses and if not then are they considered Muktzah?

_____

_____

Is a handle which has fallen off a door Muktzah?

_____

_____

If a screen or window came out of its sockets may they be returned to them and if not are they Muktzah?

_____

_____

Is a hand or pocket watch which has stopped considered Muktzah:

_____

_____

Is a Pasul pair of Tzitzis Muktzah?

_____

_____

Is a new Tallis which has not yet had its Tzitzis woven into them Muktzah?

_____

_____

Are new detached fringes for Tzitzis Muktzah?

_____

_____

12. Moving vessels which are made up, or appear to be made up, of assembled parts:

_____

_____

13-15 Moving an item which contains a Muktzah item on it:

13. The laws of a Basis:

A. The conditions required to define an item as a Basis:

_____

_____

B. The law of a Basis when the Muktzah item was removed from it on Shabbos after Bein Hashmashos:

_____

_____

Shabbos Workbook

Additional Notes

Shabbos Workbook

Q&A

What is the definition of "forgetting" a Muktzah object on a non-Muktzah support?

If a member of one's household placed a Muktzah object on a non-Muktzah item is it considered a Basis?

If the owner of the non-Muktzah item saw one placing a Muktzah item on it and did not protest?

Does food which had a Muktzah item intentionally placed on it from before Shabbos become Muktzah?

If a MM"I object was placed on Non-Muktzah item does that item become a Basis?

If a Non-Muktzah item is resting over a Muktzah item does that Non-Muktzah become a Basis?

If the Muktzah and non-Muktzah object have the same value, does the Basis still become Muktzah?

If a more important non-Muktzah object was placed on the Basis without intention for it to be there on Shabbos, or with intention to remove before Shabbos and later forgot, can it still have the power to make the Basis non-Muktzah, despite that the Muktzah object was placed intentionally?

If one had in mind to place the more important non-Muktzah item on the Basis before Shabbos, and forgot to do so, is the Muktzah object considered forgotten thus making the Basis not Muktzah?

Shabbos Workbook

If one placed the more important non-Muktzah item on the Basis before Shabbos with intention to remove on Shabbos does the Basis become Muktzah?

Additional Notes

Shabbos Workbook

Is the importance of the objects measured in accordance to its value or in accordance to its necessity?

_____

_____

What type of Non-Muktzah item helps to be placed on a table with lit candlesticks, to allow moving the table on Shabbos?

_____

_____

If one knows he will want to move the Basis on Shabbos with the non-Muktzah item should he remove the Muktzah item from before Shabbos in order so he not need to shake it off?

_____

_____

If a Muktzah item and its Basis are on a surface, must the non-Muktzah item be of greater value then both the Muktzah item and its Basis?

_____

_____

If one accepts Shabbos early, must the non-Muktzah item be on the table from when he accepts Shabbos?

_____

_____

If a Muktzah item was intentionally placed on a Sefer Torah does it become a Basis?

_____

_____

If a Muktzah item was intentionally placed on a Sefer does that Sefer become Muktzah?

_____

_____

14. Moving a non-Basis item that has a Muktzah item on it:
A. For the sake of the Muktzah object

_____

_____

B. For the sake of the Non-Muktzah item or to use its space:

_____

_____

15. Examples of a Basis, and the movement of items that are not a Basis:
A. Examples brought in the rules mentioned in Halacha 13-15:

_____

Shabbos Workbook

Additional Notes

Shabbos Workbook

B. The law of a nest that has an egg inside of it:

_____

_____

C. A door with a candle or other Muktzah object attached to it:

_____

_____

May one open the door of fridge with Muktzah items on it?

_____

_____

D. Moving candles, candle sticks, lamps and candelabras lit from before Shabbos:

_____

_____

E. Moving a tray or table with a candle on it:
One forgot to remove the candle from the tray from before Shabbos and it is thus not a Basis:

_____

_____

If one intentionally left the candle on the tray:

_____

_____

Q&A
May one before Shabbos place bread or another permitted item on a candle tray to allow moving it on Shabbos?

_____

_____

What type of Non-Muktzah item helps to be placed on a table with lit candlesticks, to allow moving the table on Shabbos?

_____

_____

If candles on a tray were placed on a table and no Non-Muktzah item of greater value was placed on the tray or table, does the tray and table become Muktzah?

_____

_____

If a permitted item of greater value was placed on the table but not the tray is the tray nevertheless Muktzah?

_____

_____

Shabbos Workbook

Additional Notes

Shabbos Workbook

In a case that the table has become Muktzah may one eat on the table?

_____

_____

F. The laws of moving leftovers from ones table:
 May one remove leftover bones and peels from ones table?

_____

_____

May one move the table or tablecloth together with the shells and place them elsewhere?

_____

_____

May one move the actual table if he cannot shake off the peels?

_____

_____

Q&A

May one remove the inedible from the food before he places it in his mouth?

_____

_____

May one place bread on a table with inedible foods in order to be allowed to remove the table together with the inedible, or must the bread be there before the inedible foods were placed on the table?

_____

_____

May items other than bread which are placed on the table also allow one to move the tablecloth?

_____

_____

G. Moving a casing of knives which has a Muktzah knife inside of it:

_____

_____

H. May one move an item that has a stone inserted into it?

_____

_____

I. Moving an item which has a stone or money on top of it:

_____

_____

Shabbos Workbook

<u>Additional Notes</u>

Shabbos Workbook

J. Clothing that have a Muktzah item in their pouch/pocket:

_____

_____

Q&A

If one remembered that he is carrying a Muktzah item in his pocket or on his belt and dropping it does not involve loss, may he nevertheless bring it to a desired area?

_____

_____

One who found a Muktzah object in his Shabbos pants, shirt, or suit jacket what is he to do?

_____

_____

K. A table with a draw that contains Muktzah items in it:

_____

_____

Q&A

If a table became a Basis for a Muktzah object, may its drawers nevertheless still be opened and closed?

_____

_____

If one left some coins in a drawer on the Shabbos table does the table become Muktzah as a result?

_____

_____

L. Removing an insulated radish from amongst earth:

_____

_____

M. A box or bag that has Muktzah and Non-Muktzah items inside it:

_____

_____

What is the law of a set of keys which contains Muktzah keys on it?

_____

_____

16. May one lift up a child that has a Muktzah object in his hand?
A. When the child has a stone in his hand:

_____

_____

Shabbos Workbook

Additional Notes

Shabbos Workbook

B. When the child has money in his hand:

_____

_____

17. The law of Nolad:
A. The stringent opinion by Nolad, its definition and the Final Ruling:

_____

_____

B. What is the status of an item that was turned into a vessel on Shabbos by a gentile?

_____

_____

C. Vessels that broke on Shabbos and are now fit for a new use:

_____

_____

D. Leftover bones and peels?

_____

_____

E. A great form of Nolad:

_____

_____

F. Is rainwater considered Nolad?

_____

_____

Q&A

Is snow Muktzah?

_____

_____

May one move a bucket of water which has leaked from an air conditioner?

_____

_____

18. The law of Muktzah on Yom Tov:
A. The laws of Muktzah relevant on Yom Tov in contrast to Shabbos:

_____

_____

Shabbos Workbook

Additional Notes

Shabbos Workbook

Q&A

When Yom Tov falls on Shabbos do the Muktzah laws follow the leniencies of the laws of Shabbos?

_____

_____

Is melting fat or ice on Yom Tov also forbidden due to the Nolad prohibition which applies on Yom Tov?

_____

_____

May one make ice cubes, freeze ice cream and the like on Yom Tov?

_____

_____

B. Moving Muktzah for eating purposes:

_____

_____

Q&A

May one kick a Muktzah item in order to make a use of it, such as to kick a rock to where the pot is sitting?

_____

_____

May one move a Muktzah item which is interfering with him doing other Yom Tov permitted matters?

_____

_____

May one move a Muktzah item which is interfering even if he could have done so from before Yom Tov?

_____

_____

May one move the interfering Muktzah object in a regular way if he can also do so using an irregularity?

_____

_____

If a Muktzah item was purposely left on a food from before Yom Tov does the food become a Basis?

_____

_____

Shabbos Workbook

<u>Additional Notes</u>

Shabbos Workbook

Chapter 2: Using Muktzah materials to clean oneself from a bowel movement

1. Using stones to wipe oneself with:

A. When having a bowel movement in an open area:

_____

_____

B. The law by a private bathroom used only by oneself:

_____

_____

C. Carrying stones to clean oneself with, within a Karmalis and Public domain:

_____

_____

D. Removing the stones from mud:

_____

_____

E. Using a stone that has mold growing on it:

_____

_____

E. May one smoothen the stone on Shabbos?

_____

_____

F. Until what point in cleanliness may one use the rocks to clean himself?

_____

_____

2. Using other Muktzah materials to wipe oneself with

A. Using a piece of earth to clean oneself with:

_____

_____

B. Cleaning oneself using pieces of pottery:

_____

_____

C. Using blades of grass over using stones:

Shabbos Workbook

Additional Notes

Shabbos Workbook

D. May one use a tree to wipe if he has nothing else available?

_____

_____

3. Miscellaneous laws involved with a bowel movement on Shabbos
A. Rubbing a stone on ones skin to treat constipation:

_____

_____

B. Making a bowel movement in a plowed field:

_____

_____

C. Making oneself a toilet out from stones

_____

_____

Q&A
May one cut the toilet paper on Shabbos if he has no precut toilet paper from before Shabbos?

_____

_____

May one use paper to wipe himself with if he has nothing else available?

_____

_____

Chapter 3: The laws relating to moving a corpse on Shabbos

1. Saving a dead body from a fire:
A. The problem of Muktzah:

_____

_____

B. The problem of carrying it in an area without an Eiruv:

_____

_____

2. Moving the body to prevent it from erosion:
A. The problem of Muktzah:

_____

_____

Shabbos Workbook

Additional Notes

Shabbos Workbook

B. The problem of carrying it in an area without an Eiruv:

_____

_____

C. Making a tent over the corpse to protect it from the sun

_____

_____

3. Moving the body in order to remove its odor from the house

_____

_____

4. Moving the body out of respect for the dead:

_____

_____

Transgressing Shabbos in order to save a body from autopsy

_____

_____

5. May one move the body for purpose that does not involve its respect?

_____

_____

6. Laws regarding moving the body with a permitted item on it, in cases explained above that it is allowed

_____

_____

7. Washing and spreading ointment over the corpse:

_____

_____

8. Closing its mouth and eyes:

_____

_____

Chapter 4: Laws relevant to insulating food before Shabbos with Muktzah materials

1. What does one do if he insulated using a Muktzah material?

_____

_____

Shabbos Workbook

2. What does one do if also the cover of the pot is Muktzah?

_____

_____

3. Rocks and wood that are placed around the oven:

_____

_____

<u>Additional Notes</u>

Shabbos Workbook

Shabbos Workbook

A Semicha aid for learning:

The laws of Shabbos

Workbook

Volume 2
Shulchan Aruch Chapters 313-317; 319-330

This Volume includes the Laws of:

Building
Cutting and Tearing
Smearing
Ohel
Trapping/Killing
Tying
Borer
Winnowing
Squeezing
Melting
Molid Reiach
Dyeing
Salting
Grinding
Kneading
Bathing
Medicine

Compiled by Rabbi Yaakov Goldstein

Shabbos Workbook

The laws of building and destroying:

Chapter 1: Makeh Bepatish-Tikkun Keli: Fixing or building an item on Shabbos

1. The definition of the prohibition

_____

_____

2. Examples of fixings that involve Tikkun Keli:
A. Removing cloth balls and straw from ones clothing:

_____

_____

B. Making a design on a vessel:

_____

_____

C. Placing stuffing into a pillow

_____

_____

D. Fixing a needle

_____

_____

E. Inserting straps into clothing

_____

_____

F. Inserting a door into vessels that do not hold 40 Seah and are not attached to the ground:

_____

_____

Q&A

May one attach the wool lining to a coat?

_____

_____

May one place shoelaces on his shoes on Shabbos?

_____

_____

Shabbos Workbook

<u>Additional Notes</u>

Shabbos Workbook

May one inflate a ball, tire, mattress with air on Shabbos?

May one inflate a balloon?

May one inflate using a mechanical pump?

May one make a necklace or bracelet by entering items into them?

May one use wax earplugs on Shabbos which are required to be shaped to fit into one's ear?

---

3. Cutting, tearing, or breaking an item in order to make a use with it:

---

4. Examples of cutting and breaking which involve Tikkun Keli:

A. Tearing an item in the process of barbecuing fish on Yom Tov

---

B. Cutting a vine to fit a use:

C. May one remove a reed from ones broom

D. Using a twig as a tooth pick

Shabbos Workbook

Additional Notes

Shabbos Workbook

E. Plucking a leaf from a branch to use as a funnel:

F. Cutting a knot

G. Cutting and tearing sewn threads

H. Tearing the covering off of a bottle

Q&A

May one separate two plastic spoons which are attached or two yogurts which are attached?

May one separate a two part ices?

5. Tikkun Keli by foods

6. The laws of puncturing a hole into a vessel on Shabbos:
A. The Biblical prohibition

B. The Rabbinical prohibition in making a hole for entering or exiting

7. Making a hole in a barrel:
A. Chopping off the top of a barrel

Shabbos Workbook

Additional Notes

Shabbos Workbook

B. The prohibition to make a hole in the side of the barrel

_____

_____

C. Making a hole in the lid of a barrel

_____

_____

Q&A

May one use a corkscrew to remove the cork of a bottle?

_____

_____

8. Doing an action which causes a hole to be made unintentionally:
A. Removing a knife from a barrel

_____

_____

B. Removing a knife from a bench and the like

_____

_____

9. Unplugging the hole of a barrel of wine

_____

_____

10. Using a tool to drill a hole through a plugged up hole of a vessel

_____

_____

11. May one unplug a drainage pipe on Shabbos?

_____

_____

12. The prohibition of plugging a hole on Shabbos

_____

_____

13. Inserting a tap into the hole of a barrel on Shabbos:

_____

_____

Shabbos Workbook

Additional Notes

Shabbos Workbook

Chapter 2: The building and destroying prohibition:

1. The general rules of the prohibition:
A. Items attached to the ground

B. Vessels that are not attached to the ground but are large enough to hold 40 Seah

C. Vessels that are not attached to the ground and are not large enough to hold 40 Seah

D. Destroying not for the sake of building a better building:

Halachas 2-5: The laws of Assembling and Disassembling the parts of a vessel:

2. Inserting or removing the door of a vessels attached to the ground or which hold 40 seah:
A. Returning or removing the door of a pit, or of a vessel attached to the ground, to or from its hinges

B. Removing the doors of vessels which hold 40 seah

C. Removing a door of a pit which is not on hinges

3. Inserting a door into vessels that do not hold 40 Seah and are not attached to the ground:
A. By doors that have hinges on their top and bottom as opposed to their side

B. By doors with a hinge on their side

Shabbos Workbook

<u>Additional Notes</u>

Shabbos Workbook

4. Removing doors from vessels that are not attached to the ground and do not hold 40 Seah

_____

_____

5. Assembling and disassembling vessels [that do not hold 40 Seah and are not attached to the ground]:
A. Assembling parts firmly:

_____

_____

B. Disassembling parts that are firmly attached

_____

_____

C. Assembling parts together semi-firmly

_____

_____

D. Disassembling parts that are semi-firmly attached

_____

_____

E. Assembling the parts completely loose

_____

_____

F. Muktzah decrees made due to prohibition to reinsert firmly

_____

_____

Q&A

May one adjust the height of a shtender on Shabbos?

_____

_____

May one attach a table extender to his table on Shabbos?

_____

_____

May a child play building games such as Lego and the like?

_____

_____

Shabbos Workbook

Additional Notes

Shabbos Workbook

May one form a ship, plane, and the like from [non-Muktzah] paper?

_____

_____

May one make napkin designs for the Shabbos table setting?

_____

_____

May one fix broken glasses?

_____

_____

May one fix a baby stroller?

_____

_____

May one insert or remove the seat of a baby walker?

_____

_____

May one oil the squeaky hinges of an item?

_____

_____

Halachos 6-9: The laws of breaking a vessel on Shabbos

6 . Breaking an incomplete [non-sturdy] vessel on Shabbos

_____

_____

7. The prohibition to break a complete/sturdy vessel on Shabbos

_____

_____

8. Breaking vessels that are attached to the ground:
A. Breaking the ropes that tie a door to a pit

_____

_____

B. Breaking the clay off from the opening of the oven which has been plastered shut

_____

_____

Shabbos Workbook

<u>Additional Notes</u>

Shabbos Workbook

9. Examples:

_____

_____

Q&A

May one open cans of food on Shabbos?

_____

_____

May one open a can of soda?

_____

_____

May one open a can using its easy open lid?

_____

_____

May one break open wrappers which contain food or any other sealed bag in order to get to its content?

_____

_____

May one remove or make a hole in the covering of an item such as yogurt, wine bottle and the like?

_____

_____

May one remove the caps of bottles such as soda or wine bottle?

_____

_____

May one remove the metal/plastic strip of a cover of a container or bottle, to thus be able to open it?

_____

_____

May one break the top of a bottle if he is not able to remove the cap?

_____

_____

May one open an envelope on Shabbos?

_____

_____

Shabbos Workbook

<u>Additional Notes</u>

Shabbos Workbook

Halachas 10-15: Miscellaneous cases which may involve the Building prohibition

10. The Biblical Prohibition to make a hole in a wall, floor, or vessel which holds 40 Seah:

A. The general rule:

B. Removing a knife from a wall

Q&A

May one enter a nail or other item into an already existing hole?

May one attach a wall hanger or hook to his wall or door on Shabbos?

11. Placing an item to support the beam of a roof that is caving inwards

12. Placing an item to support the broken leg of a couch or bench and the like

13. Leveling the floor and the ground

14. The laws of smearing saliva on the ground

15. May one gather non-Muktzah rocks and use it to build a temporary structure

Shabbos Workbook

Additional Notes

Shabbos Workbook

Chapter 3: Laws which relate to inserting or removing windows, shutters, doors and locks on Shabbos

1. Inserting a shutter, windowpane or screen into a window

2. Removing the window frame from the window of the house

3. Inserting or removing a door into or from an opening/doorway
1. Returning or removing a door into or from its hinges:

2. Placing a door by an opening without placing it on hinges:
A. Openings that are only sporadically used for entering and exiting from:

B. Openings that are constantly used for entering and exiting

C. Inserting doors into openings that do not have a threshold

D. Placing a door made of a single plank of wood into a doorway

4. Inserting a lock onto ones door

5. Barricading ones door using a bolt or rod:
A. Barricading ones door with a wooden rod:

Shabbos Workbook

Additional Notes

Shabbos Workbook

6. Locking ones door with placing a peg in the doorstep behind the door:
A. The law by a peg without a handle

B. How does one tie the peg?

C. A peg that inserts into the ground:

D. Locking with a peg which had a handle inserted into it:

Shabbos Workbook

<u>Additional Notes</u>

Shabbos Workbook

The laws of cutting and tearing:

Prohibition #1: The/Koreah/Tearing prohibition
The laws of Tearing sewn items and separating glued items on Shabbos

1. The rules of the prohibition and when it applies:
A. The Principal prohibition-Tearing with intent to re-sew:

_____

_____

B. Tearing without intent to re-sew:

_____

_____

C. Tearing with intent to sew but not in a better way than done originally:

_____

_____

D. Prohibition only applies by tearing apart many entities:

_____

_____

E. The law if the sewing was only meant to last temporarily:

_____

_____

2. Tearing leather:

_____

_____

3. Separating papers and other items that are glued together:

_____

_____

Q&A
May one separate items that were intentionally glued for temporary use?

_____

_____

May one cut attached pages of a new book which were forgotten to be cut during the binding?

_____

_____

Shabbos Workbook

Additional Notes

Shabbos Workbook

May one tear glued pages of a book if doing so will tear some of the letters or the paper?

_____

_____

May one place a band-aid on a wound on Shabbos?

_____

_____

May one use diapers on Shabbos which are fastened using a piece of tape or Velcro which is attached to the diaper?

_____

_____

4. Cutting and tearing threads sewn in for temporary use, such as to attach a pair of shoes together:

_____

_____

5. Removing entangled clothing from thorns:

_____

_____

6. Breaking an almond using a cloth:

_____

_____

<u>Prohibition # 2: Tikkun Keli-Fixing an item for a usage in the process of cutting it</u>

1. Cutting an item to make a use for it:

_____

_____

2. Breaking earthenware and tearing paper for a use:

_____

_____

3. Cutting a hole into a vessel:

_____

_____

4. Examples of cases which involve fixing a vessel:
A. Tearing an item in the process of barbecuing fish on Yom Tov:

_____

_____

Shabbos Workbook

Additional Notes

Shabbos Workbook

B. Cutting a vine to fit a use:

_____

_____

C. May one remove a reed from ones broom?

_____

_____

D. Using a twig as a tooth pick:

_____

_____

E. Cutting a knot

_____

_____

5. Tikkun Keli by foods:

_____

_____

Q&A
May one fix a vessel through using food parts, such as to carve a piece of vegetable to be fit to be used as a funnel for a barrel?

_____

_____

Prohibition # 3: Michateich-The prohibition of cutting an item to a required size

1. The principal prohibition:

_____

_____

2. The offshoot prohibition:

_____

_____

3. Examples:

_____

_____

Shabbos Workbook

Additional Notes

Shabbos Workbook

Prohibition # 4: The prohibition of cutting an item to small pieces

1. The prohibition to cut an item into small pieces:

_____

_____

Prohibition # 5: The prohibition of doing a Mundane act

1. The prohibition of doing a mundane act even if no actual prohibited work is involved:

_____

_____

Prohibition #6: The Destroying prohibition

One may only destroy a vessel [as opposed to disassemble] if:

_____

_____

Prohibition # 7: The prohibition against erasing letters

One may never cut or tear an item with lettering or pictures in a way that the letters or pictures become ruined.

_____

_____

Cases of tearing which do not contain any prohibition:
1. The conditions needed to be allowed to cut an item on Shabbos:

_____

_____

2. Cutting the strings wrapped or sewed around food:

_____

_____

3. Breaking the rope that secures a cover to its vessel:

_____

_____

4. The prohibition to break a lock on Shabbos:

_____

_____

5. Breaking through woven palm leaf baskets in order to get the food inside:

_____

_____

Shabbos Workbook

<u>Additional Notes</u>

Shabbos Workbook

6. Breaking the ropes that tie a door to a pit:

_____

_____

May one cut an item on Shabbos?

_____

_____

Practical Q&A

May one tear a piece of cotton from a cotton ball or cotton sheet?

_____

_____

May one tear toilet paper?

_____

_____

May one separate plastic ware which is attached together, such as two plastic spoons which are attached or two yogurts which are attached?

_____

_____

May one separate a two part ices?

_____

_____

May one open up an envelope?

_____

_____

May one place a band-aid on a wound on Shabbos?

_____

_____

May one use diapers on Shabbos which are fastened using a piece of tape or Velcro which is attached to the diaper?

_____

_____

May one cut a piece of tape?

_____

_____

158

Shabbos Workbook

May one cut or tear a bandage to make it a better fit?

Additional Notes

Shabbos Workbook

Laws of Mimacheik/Smearing:

The smearing prohibition "Mimacheik"

1. The general Law:

_____

_____

2. Spreading and smoothening foods on Shabbos:

_____

_____

Q&A

If the food is unable to be eaten unless one spreads the food on it, may it nevertheless be spread on it?

_____

_____

May one smoothen the top of a dip such as Chumus, Tehina, mashed potatoes?

_____

_____

May one smoothen and spread cooked apples onto bread?

_____

_____

May one spread butter onto his bread?

_____

_____

May one smear icing onto cake on Shabbos?

_____

_____

May one spread cream on a cake using an icing tip to form designs?

_____

_____

3. Smearing fat and oil:

_____

_____

Shabbos Workbook

4. The laws of smearing saliva on the ground:

_____

_____

<u>Additional Notes</u>

Shabbos Workbook

Q&A

Does washing ones hands with a bar of soap contain the smoothening prohibition [Mimacheik]?
May one smear a cream onto ones skin?

_____

_____

May one dab a cream on one's body without smearing it?

_____

_____

May one apply Vaseline to dry lips on Shabbos?

_____

_____

May one remove wax blotches [as well as other forms of blotches] from letters of a Sefer Torah and does it invalidate the Torah?

_____

_____

May one remove glue from one's skin on Shabbos?

_____

_____

May one enter ear plugs into his ears on Shabbos?

_____

_____

May one play with play dough and the like on Shabbos?

_____

Shabbos Workbook

Additional Notes

Shabbos Workbook

The Laws of making an Ohel:

1. Putting up a roofing/hovering for protection purposes
A. To initially open a hovering on Shabbos

_____

_____

B. To further open a hovering that was opened from before Shabbos:

_____

_____

C. Examples:
Placing mats over the frames of a roof:

_____

_____

Spreading a sheet over a baby's crib:

_____

_____

Making a tent over the corpse to protect it from the sun:

_____

_____

Making oneself a toilet out from stones:

_____

_____

May one open or close the roofing of a Sukkah?

_____

_____

Q&A

May one hold up a hovering using his hands?

_____

_____

Does roof netting have the same law as does a sheet?

_____

_____

Shabbos Workbook

Additional Notes

Shabbos Workbook

May one on Shabbos set up non-Muktzah panels within three handbreadths of each other?

_____

_____

May people hold open a sheet or a Tallis to grant shade or protection from rain?

_____

_____

On Simchas Torah may people spread open a Tallis over the Chasan Torah and children by Kol Nearim?

_____

_____

May one open or close a rain umbrella on Shabbos?

_____

_____

May one use an umbrella that was opened from before Shabbos?

_____

_____

May one open a sun umbrella?

_____

_____

May one open or close a sun roof or roof window?

_____

_____

May one open or close an umbrella which extends past the roof of one's house?

_____

_____

May one place netting over a crib or ones bed to protect it from insects?

_____

_____

May one open the hood of a baby carriage on Shabbos?

_____

_____

Shabbos Workbook

May one spread a sun or rain cover over a baby carriage on Shabbos?

<u>**Additional Notes**</u>

Shabbos Workbook

May one open an umbrella that is attached to a stroller from before Shabbos?

_____

_____

May one form a plastic stroller covering like a tent, over the floor, from before Shabbos and place it on his stroller on Shabbos if need be?

_____

_____

2. Making roofing for non protection purposes:
A. If there is no walls under the roofing item:

_____

_____

B. If there is walls/boards under the roofing item:

_____

_____

C. Examples:
Placing a board, sheet or mattress on top of a bed frame:

_____

_____

Setting up barrels:

_____

_____

Setting up books:

_____

_____

Setting up a table on its walled legs:

_____

_____

A folding chair:

_____

_____

Setting up a wedding canopy:

_____

_____

Shabbos Workbook

Additional Notes

Shabbos Workbook

Opening and closing a shelf:

_____

_____

Setting up a strainer:

_____

_____

Examples which relate to setting up fire places on Yom Tov:

_____

_____

D. Making roofing on walls which were set up from before Shabbos-Such as placing and removing the cover of a vessel:

_____

_____

Practical Q&A

May one open or close a folding chair, table, bed, stroller, and crib on Shabbos?

_____

_____

May one place a mattress over his bed on Shabbos?

_____

_____

May one add an extension to ones table on Shabbos?

_____

_____

May one insert/remove a drawer into/from a desk or table?

_____

_____

3. Mantling tented roofing on Shabbos:
A. The law:

_____

_____

B. Initially spreading a sheet and the like over a bar on Shabbos:

_____

_____

Shabbos Workbook

<u>Additional Notes</u>

Shabbos Workbook

C. Opening a sheet that was wrapped on a bar from before Shabbos in order to form a tent:

_____

_____

D. Spreading a sheet over the bar of the bed canopy of a groom:

_____

_____

4. Dismantling roofing on Shabbos:

_____

_____

Q&A
May one dismantle roofing which was spread from before Shabbos up to a handbreadth of the roofing?

_____

_____

5. Wearing Shabbos hats, sun hats, baseball caps etc. on Shabbos:
A. Wearing a hat with an extension for protection purposes:

_____

_____

B. Wearing a hat with an extension not for protection purposes:

_____

_____

Q&A
May one wear a baseball cap on Shabbos?

_____

_____

May one wear a Shabbos hat?

_____

_____

6. Setting up dividers [makeshift walls] on Shabbos:
A. The prohibition to make a permanent divider:

_____

_____

B. Setting up a temporary divider for shade, privacy, to prevent cold and similar purposes:

_____

_____

Shabbos Workbook

Additional Notes

Shabbos Workbook

C. Setting up temporary dividers to separate domains and thus remove a prohibition:

_____

_____

D. Adding to an already existing divider:

_____

_____

E. Hanging sheets and other items that move in the wind as a separation:

_____

_____

Q&A

May one set up a temporary divider if it is usually meant to be left as a permanent divider?

_____

_____

May one set up a divider for privacy reasons if it will later serve also to Halachicly divide the room?

_____

_____

May one undo a divider which served to Halachicly divide the room?

_____

_____

May one open or close a folding wall Mechitzah of a Shul?

_____

_____

Shabbos Workbook

Additional Notes

Shabbos Workbook

The Laws of Trapping and Killing animals, birds and insects on Shabbos:

Chapter 1: The laws of Trapping creatures on Shabbos

1. The Principal Prohibition:

_____

_____

2. The Biblical Prohibition:
A. One completely traps the creature:

_____

_____

B. One traps for self use as opposed to trapping to prevent injury:

_____

_____

C. Trapping something which is not commonly trapped being that it serves no use:

_____

_____

D. The animal is not old or crippled:

_____

_____

E. The trapping was done singlehandedly if possible:

_____

_____

F. The creature is not one's pet or farm animal:

_____

_____

3. The Rabbinical prohibition of trapping:

_____

_____

Q&A
May one enter a creature from outside a house to inside the house if he leaves the door open, or another obvious escape route for the creature?

_____

_____

Shabbos Workbook

Additional Notes

Shabbos Workbook

May one trap an animal that is never commonly trapped and can never run away, such as a turtle and ant?

_____

_____

Is there a prohibition involved in trapping humans, such as locking a child in his room, or a lunatic into his room?

_____

_____

4. A mouse trap - Setting up a trap mechanism on and before Shabbos :
A. Setting up a trap from before Shabbos to trap on Shabbos:

_____

_____

B. Setting up a trap on Shabbos:

_____

_____

5. Hunting dogs:

_____

_____

6. Un-trapping an animal on Shabbos

_____

_____

7. One who unintentionally trapped a creature:

_____

_____

8. Closing the door of one's house when he knows an animal or bird is inside:

_____

_____

9. Locking the closed door of a room which contains an animal:

_____

_____

10. Using one's body to block the exit of a room that contains an animal:

_____

_____

Shabbos Workbook

Additional Notes

Shabbos Workbook

11. Covering a vessel that has flies or other flying insects in it:

12. Covering a beehive in order to protect it from damage:

13. Trapping pets and farm animals:
A. The Biblical Prohibition-Trapping rebellious pets and farm animals:

B. The Rabbinical prohibition- Trapping domestic birds and wild natured animals:

C. Trapping pet birds or wild natured animals from an already trapped area:

D. Trapping pet birds or wild natured animals from one large area to another large area:

E. Trapping calm natured pets and farm animals:

F. Trapping pet Cat's:

14. Trapping to prevent injury
A. Initially trapping creeping creatures which can cause bodily injury [in contrast to mere pain]:

B. Trapping insects and the like which only cause pain:

Shabbos Workbook

<u>Additional Notes</u>

Shabbos Workbook

C. Removing an insect that is in the midst of stinging:

_____

_____

Q&A
May one trap a hornet which is disturbing ones Shabbos meal?

_____

_____

Chapter 2: Killing or injuring creatures on Shabbos

1. The Primary Melacha that was in the Tabernacle-Slaughtering:

_____

_____

2. The Biblical Prohibitions included in the above principal Melacha:
A. Killing in forms other than slaughtering:

_____

_____

B. Injuring a creature:

_____

_____

C. Killing or injuring not for a use of the creature itself:

_____

_____

D. The killing of creatures which do not reproduce-Fleas and Lice:

_____

_____

3. The Rabbinical prohibition

_____

_____

4. The killing of creatures which do not reproduce-Fleas and Lice:

_____

_____

Q&A
May one today kill lice even though we see with our own eyes that it lays eggs?

_____

Shabbos Workbook

Additional Notes

Shabbos Workbook

5. Removing a fish from water

_____

_____

6. Killing dangerous animals and creatures:
A. Creatures that definitively have a deadly bite or sting:

_____

_____

B. Creatures which are not deadly but cause bodily injury [in contrast to mere pain]:

_____

_____

C. Killing creatures which at times can be deadly and at times not that are not chasing after oneself:

_____

_____

7. The prohibition to kill insects which cause mere pain even in the midst of a bite:

_____

_____

8. Killing spiders:

_____

_____

9. Being cautious not to trample on ants and other non-dangerous creatures:

_____

_____

Practical Q&A

May one spray pesticide in his house if insects have become a nuisance to him?

_____

_____

May one place poison on the floor to kill roaches and mice on Shabbos?

_____

_____

If there are insects in ones toilet may he flush it on Shabbos after using it?

_____

_____

Shabbos Workbook

May one place on himself in the house a spray that has a bad smell and will cause the insects to leave?

_____

_____

May one wash off the pesticide, bugs, or dirt off of a fruit or vegetable?

_____

_____

Additional Notes

Shabbos Workbook

The Laws of Tying and Untying Knots On Shabbos:

1. The Biblical prohibition of tying a permanent knot:
A. The Principal Prohibition that was in the Mishkan:

B. First Opinion

C. Second Opinion:

2. The Rabbinical prohibition of tying a knot and the knots which are permitted to be tied and untied:

3. Tying and untying a double knot on Shabbos:

4. A bow knot and a single knot

5. Making a knot for the sake of a Mitzvah

6. Examples of Cases:

Untying the rope that secures a cover to its vessel:

Shabbos Workbook

Additional Notes

Shabbos Workbook

Q&A

May a knot with a bow on top be made on a disposable bag or the like which one plans to throw out and never actually undo?

_____

_____

If a professional knot occurred on its own, like strings became tangled and formed a double knot, or a bow over a knot became a double knot, may one open it on Shabbos?

_____

_____

May one make a bow on top of a bow?

_____

_____

May one make a single bow to last forever?

_____

_____

May one tie a Gartel to a Sefer Torah?

_____

_____

If one took out the Sefer Torah and found that it was tied with a double knot may it be undone?

_____

_____

May one make a tie on Shabbos?

_____

_____

May one tighten his Tzitzis on Shabbos?

_____

_____

May one tie or untie a loose double knot?

_____

_____

May one tie a scarf around his neck, or a tichel on ones hair?

Shabbos Workbook

May one tie a bandage onto a wound?

7. Cutting a knot:

8. Cutting and tearing sewn threads:

9. Weaving and unraveling ropes and wicks:

Q&A

May one wind or unwind twist-ties on Shabbos?

<u>Additional Notes</u>

Shabbos Workbook

The Laws of Borer: Separating, Peeling, And Filtering on Shabbos:

Q&A on the definition of a mixture

1. How close to each other must the pieces be, and are the most outer pieces considered mixed:

A. If a mixture has scattered do the Borer restrictions still apply?

_____

_____

B. May one purposely cause a mixture to become scattered in order so it loses its mixture definition and then be allowed to separate from it the unwanted parts?

_____

_____

C. If two pieces are sitting side by side are they considered mixed?

_____

_____

D. Are the outer pieces of a side by side mixture subject to the Borer restrictions?

_____

_____

E. If one has a basket of fruits and on the bottom lies a rotten fruit which he wants to separate does the Borer restriction apply?

_____

_____

F. May one remove the empty bottles from a table which also contains full bottles?

_____

_____

G. Does the Borer restrictions apply to removing bottles from a box which contains various bottles of juice or empty bottles?

_____

_____

2. Are two pieces which are lying on top of each other considered mixed?

A. Removing insects from on top of fruits:

_____

_____

3. Mixtures of a solid within a liquid

A. Do the Borer restrictions apply to solids which are within liquids, such as a Matzah ball within a soup?

_____

_____

Shabbos Workbook

Additional Notes

Shabbos Workbook

B. May one pour out the oil from a sardine can?

_____

_____

The laws in Shulchan Aruch

1. The Biblical Prohibition of Separating:
A. The General law:

_____

_____

B. May one remove the bad together with some of the good thus leaving the remainder of the mixture free of the bad?

_____

_____

C. May one blow away waste from amongst food?

_____

_____

D. May one soak food with its waste into water in order to separate and remove the waste ?

_____

_____

Q&A on B/C
If one will separate only some of the bad together with good and will thus still leave some of the bad with the mixture do the Borer regulations still apply?

_____

_____

May one blow the nut shells and chaff away from a grouping of opened nuts, as is common with opened peanuts which have their chaff [the brown thin shelling] mixed in with them?

_____

_____

Q&A on soaking foods in water:
May one soak foods in order to remove waste that majority of people are not particular to wash off?

_____

_____

If the food was already within the water from before Shabbos may one rub it off on Shabbos?

_____

_____

Shabbos Workbook

May one soak a fruit or vegetable in order to remove the pesticide, bugs, or dirt off of the fruit or vegetable?

May one wash off waste from foods that majority of people are not particular to wash off?

May one rinse away the waste from a mixture of food and waste?

May one wash off the pesticide, bugs, or dirt off of a fruit or vegetable?

May one use soap and the like to wash foods:

General Q&A

May one separate the bad from the good using a Shinui/irregularity?

If one will not separate all the bad from the good or vice versa, and thus will still be left with a mixture of some bad and good do the Borer regulations still apply?

What is the law if one accidently did Borer on Shabbos, may the food still be eaten?

If one accidently removed the waste from the mixture, such as he removed a fruit from a pile, and the fruit was rotten does he need to replace the fruit back into the mixture?

May one remove waste from waste, such as to remove peels of Kedushas Shevias away from other waste?

Shabbos Workbook

May one separate for the purpose of verifying whether or not he has lost a certain item or not?

2. Cases which contain the Borer prohibition:
A. Making cheese on Shabbos:

B. Removing seeds and nuts from honey:

C. Catalyzing beverages on Shabbos:

Q&A
May one place lemon into milk on Shabbos to turn it into cheese?

May one place milk in a hot area on Shabbos in order to turn it into cheese?

3. The Rabbinical prohibition of Separating:

4. The Permitted method of separating

Q&A on the definition of what is considered waste/unwanted
May one for whom a certain food is considered inedible separate it for one for whom that food is considered edible, such as to separate the unwanted onions of a salad in order to give them to an onion lover?

Shabbos Workbook

Additional Notes

Shabbos Workbook

May one separate inedible items from food if his intent is to use that item for a certain purpose, such as to remove the bone of a fish in order to use as a toothpick, or to remove a bone to give to a pet dog to eat?

May one remove the waste/food that he does not want with intent to eat some of it or use it, in order to retroactively allow the separating?

If one does not want to remove the wanted food from a certain vessel, such as that he desires to serve the food in this vessel, how then is he to separate the wanted from the unwanted?

Q&A on what is considered separating "using ones hands"
May one use his hand to strain food for right away use?

May one separate the food using a fork or spoon and the like?

May one separate a solid from a liquid through lifting the solid with a spoon and tilting it against the wall of the pot, thereby draining the liquid and keeping leverage of the solid?

May one separate through tilting a cup or can and spilling out the wanted or unwanted?

May one use a nut cracker to crack nuts, thus separating them from their shell?

Q&A on separating through using a strainer
May one use a strainer spoon [a spoon with small holes made to strain the liquid of the food removed] on Shabbos to remove a food which is within liquid?

Shabbos Workbook

If a pot contains a strainer in its upper part into which the solids are placed into and it then cooks in the liquid, may one remove this strainer with solids from amongst the liquid on Shabbos?

May one rinse fruits inside of a strainer?

May one pour fruits that are within water into a strainer in order to strain the water?

List of practical Q&A cases in which it is allowed to remove the waste from the food

May one remove a tea bag from ones cup of tea or does this pose a separating prohibition?

May one remove a bag of rice from ones Chulent?

May one remove bones from fish, or must he remove the fish from the bones?

May one remove bones from meat, or must he remove the meat from the bones?

May one remove the skin from chicken/meat/fish?

May one remove the pit of a fruit, or must he remove the fruit from the pit?

May one shake inedible seeds/pits out from fruits/vegetables?

Shabbos Workbook

Does removing food labels from food, such as from bakery bread, contain the separating restrictions?

_____

_____

Does removing baking paper from cake, Kishkeh, Kugel, hotdogs, and the like contain the separating restrictions?

_____

_____

Does the removing of candy wrappers contain the separating restrictions?

_____

_____

May one remove a rotten/ wormy part of fruit/vegetable in order to eat the rest of the fruit/vegetable?

_____

_____

May one remove a worm or other bug from a fruit/vegetable?

_____

_____

5. What is the definition of separating to eat "right away"?

_____

_____

Q&A On the Definition of Right Away

If one requires a lot of time in advance to prepare for the meal and do the required separations, how long in advance may one do so?

_____

_____

May one be lenient to separate within one hour before the meal even if he does not require a full hour to do the separations?

_____

_____

May one begin separating for the meal more time than is needed prior to the meal if he will not be able for whatever reason to separate right before the meal?

_____

_____

Shabbos Workbook

When doing many preparations for the meal the separating preparations be pushed off to the very end so it be as close to the meal as possible, or may one do so even in the beginning of the required preparations?

May one separate a food in more time prior to the meal than needed if the food will be better tasting if separated this early?

Should one estimate prior to the meal how much food will be eaten and thus how much separation needs to be done or may he separate without limit so long as he intends on doing so for this meal?

May one intentionally not eat some of the separated food during the meal in order to save it for another meal?

May one separate many foods in a way that it is recognizable that he is doing so for later use if he will take a bite of each individual food right away?

May one separate fruits from amongst rotten fruits to prevent them from spoiling faster?

If one has a mixture of different spices may he separate from it a specific spice for immediate use?

May one separate clothing or a Sefer to take with him outside the house even though he does not plan to wear it or read it until later on?

May one separate prior to going to sleep medicines [which may be taken on Shabbos] in order so he can take them as soon as he awakes in middle of the night?

Shabbos Workbook

Q&A on Separating for others

May one separate the good with his hands solely for others to eat right away not having himself partaken in the food?

_____

_____

May one separate good with his hands for the sake of animals to eat right away?

_____

_____

May ones separation for the meal include also people which will only be arriving for the meal much later then its initial time?

_____

_____

May one separate more food than needed for the sake of having a large portion on the table and thus have his guests feel at ease in taking however much they want?

_____

_____

May one separate foods for the honor of his guests even if he knows that they will not be eating those foods?

_____

_____

May one separate foods on behalf of giving a snack for guests to take on their way out even though they may not eat it until later on?

_____

_____

May one separate food for kids despite the lack of knowledge of how much they will eat of the food if not at all?

_____

_____

May one separate food for the need of lending to a neighbor even though the neighbor does not plan to eat it right away?

_____

_____

Does this restriction against placing the selected food into a basket apply to other foods as well or only to fruits that have fallen into earth?

_____

_____

Shabbos Workbook

6. Does the Borer restrictions apply when separating edible foods from amongst edible foods?

A. Edible food from edible food of same species:

_____

_____

B. Edible food from edible food of different species:

_____

_____

Q&A regarding what is the definition of a same species mixture and a different species mixture? Examples of foods which are considered two different species and retain all separating restrictions:

_____

_____

May one separate a piece of fish with many bones from the other pieces of that same fish?

_____

_____

May one separate the different parts of the chicken from each other without restriction, such as to separate a thigh from a breast?

_____

_____

May one separate different sized diapers one from the other without restriction?

_____

_____

May one separate large and small bread/Matzah crumbs from each other without restriction?

_____

_____

May one separate the cream off ones piece of cake?

_____

_____

May one scrape off a dip from ones bread?

_____

_____

May one separate burnt pieces of fish and the like from the other fully edible pieces of fish?

_____

_____

Shabbos Workbook

May one separate fruits which have rotten parts on them, but are still edible from their other sides, from fully edible fruits of the same species?

_____

_____

May one cut off the burnt part of a pastry from the pastry?

_____

_____

May one remove the rotten grapes from a vine?

_____

_____

Q&A on separating from same species foods which contain a forbidden part
May one remove the Kefula area of a Matzah on Pesach or does this pose a problem of Borer?

_____

_____

May one pour out the foam of a drink?

_____

_____

May one separate the whole Matzah from broken Matzah?

_____

_____

Q&A on separating the yolk from the white:
May one separate without restriction the yolk from the white or vice versa if he also plans to eat the white?

_____

_____

Q&A that relate directly to the Halachas inside
May one separate the large pieces of all species and in the process place the large pieces of each species separately?

_____

_____

May one separate from within the same species even with a vessel?

_____

_____

Shabbos Workbook

<u>Additional Notes</u>

Shabbos Workbook

May one separate from within the same species the big pieces from the small in order to give them to two different people, the big pieces to one person and the small to another?

_____

_____

Does this restriction apply even when the rotten leaves are still attached to the lettuce head?

_____

_____

General Q&A on Separating from amongst different species

If one does not care to eat either food until later on, at which time he will eat them both at that time, may he already separate them now?

_____

_____

If one desires to eat both foods during the meal, but desires to eat one prior to the other, do the separating restrictions apply?

_____

_____

If one is interested in both foods right away may he separate them with a designated vessel?

_____

_____

Does the full regulation of "Right away" apply also when separating food that one desires to eat from food which he does not desire to eat?

_____

_____

7. Pouring food or waste out from a vessel

_____

_____

8. Removing the fat off from the surface of milk and all cases of the like such as removing dirt from on food:

_____

_____

Q&A

How much fat is one required to leave upon the surface when removing the fat due to desiring only the milk?

_____

_____

Shabbos Workbook

Additional Notes

Shabbos Workbook

May one remove the entire fat together with some of the milk if he desires to get rid of the fat and drink the milk?

_____

_____

May one use a spoon to remove the fat?

_____

_____

May one remove dirt/waste from the surface of a food, such as cream cheese and the like?

_____

_____

9. Removing a fly or other waste from ones soup or cup of juice:

_____

_____

Q&A

May one remove pieces of cork from ones wine on Shabbos?

_____

_____

May one move the fly or other waste to the side of the cup using ones hand or spoon?

_____

_____

May one blow the waste to the side even if it is covering the surface of the food to the point that it is impossible to drink it without blowing it to the side?

_____

_____

May one splash away the dirt that floats on the surface of a Mikvah?

_____

_____

10. May one remove fruits etc that have fallen into pebbles and dirt, from the floor?

_____

_____

11. Separating vessels from waste and from amongst other types of vessels?

_____

_____

Shabbos Workbook

<u>Additional Notes</u>

Shabbos Workbook

Q&A

May one separate paper with words of Torah from mundane papers in order to throw out the pile of mundane papers and place the Torah papers in genizah?

_____

_____

May one separate the different recycling items on Shabbos?

_____

_____

The laws of Borer which pertain to clothing:

The definition of a mixture to which the Borer restrictions pertain:

_____

_____

May one remove clothing from his closet or drawer in order to reach specific clothing?

_____

_____

May one remove clothing from a mixture for later use if he will not have the ability to separate the clothing right away prior to the use? Such as may one who has a mixture of clothing with his sweater take his sweater prior to leaving the house even though he does not plan on using it until later on at night when it gets cold?

_____

_____

May one separate clothing from a mixture on Friday night to have it prepared to be worn the next day on Shabbos?

_____

_____

If clothing are sitting one on top of the other on a clothing hanger may one remove the upper clothing in order to reach the lower clothing?

_____

_____

May one remove dirt/crumbs and the like from ones shtreimal or Sheitel?

_____

_____

May one shake dust and the like off a hat, Sheital?

_____

_____

Shabbos Workbook

The laws of Borer which pertain to eating utensils:

May one remove the eating utensils from their drawer in order to set up the table not immediately prior to the meal?

If the utensils are mixed may one only remove the exact amount of utensils prior to the meal?

May one remove a utensil from the mixture for the purpose of using it to save his spot on the table, or as a separating between a man and his wife?

May one separate the Milk utensils from the meat utensils and the like?

May one remove the dirty utensils from the table in order to clean the table?

After the meal may one remove the utensils from amongst the waste that is on the table?

May one remove a fork/spoon/knife that fell into a liquid?

If a vessel fell into the garbage may one remove it from the garbage without restriction?

May one sort out the utensils each one with its kind to place them now in the dish washer so they are ready for after Shabbos?

May one sort out the utensils in order to wash them separately?

Shabbos Workbook

May one sort out the utensils in order to dry them separately or place them away each one in their set spot?

_____

_____

The laws of Borer which pertain to keys:
Are keys in a key chain defined as mixed and thereby retain the separating restrictions?

_____

_____

May one separate one of the middle keys not for a right away use if he is simply holding on to it while it remains still on the key chain?

_____

_____

What is one to do if he needs to remove a middle key from the key chain to take with him when he leaves the house so he be able to open the door when he returns, but does not need to lock the door now upon him leaving, such as if people are still awake in the home?

_____

_____

The laws of Borer which pertain to books:
What is defined as a mixture of two different types of books?

_____

_____

May one gather all the Chumashim or Siddurim from the tables of the Shul in order to place them in their set place on the shelves?

_____

_____

If one has a pile of different books may he remove one book at a time and place it in its set place on the shelf?

_____

_____

If one has a pile of different books and desires to organize them on the shelf does it help if one looks into each book after separating it in order to be considered a right away use?

_____

_____

If a pile of papers from a folder got mixed up may one separate them from each other in order to organize them?

_____

_____

Shabbos Workbook

The laws of Borer that pertain to a mixture of toys/cards/games/etc.

<u>Additional Notes</u>

Shabbos Workbook

Chapter 2: The laws of Mifarek [separating grains and legumes from their peels and stalks] and peeling fruits and vegetables

1. Rubbing and peeling shells/ stalks/ pods off from nuts/seeds/beans on Shabbos:

_____

_____

Q&A

Does the Mifarek prohibition also apply to pods which are grown with intent to be marketed together with their pods?

_____

_____

May one peel off the pods of beans, peas, green beans?

_____

_____

May one remove corn from the cob on Shabbos?

_____

_____

May one break open the shells of a nut using a vessel which is specified for that purpose, such as a nut cracker?

_____

_____

May one use a hammer to break open the nut?

_____

_____

Once the shell has been cracked may one remove it from around the nut or must he remove the nut from out of the Shell?

_____

_____

May one peel off the shells of peanuts?

_____

_____

May one peel off the outer peel of garlic [the peel which contains within it all the cloves] and take apart the cloves from each other on Shabbos?

_____

_____

Shabbos Workbook

<u>Additional Notes</u>

Shabbos Workbook

According to Admur in the Siddur may one eat sunflower seeds on Shabbos?

2. Peeling fruits and vegetables:
Do the Borer restrictions [i.e. to peel for a right away use] apply even to fruits/vegetables which are edible with their peel and one just decides to peel it for whatever reason?

May one peel off the outer peel of garlic [the peel which contains within it all the cloves] and take apart the cloves from each other on Shabbos?

May one remove bananas or grapes from their vine?

May one remove the stems from fruits and vegetables?

May one peel fruits/vegetables which do not contain the separating restriction even for the need of after Shabbos?

May one use a peeler to peel fruits and vegetables on Shabbos?

May one use a knife to peel fruits and vegetables with?

If one only desires to eat part of the fruit is he nevertheless allowed to peel off the peel of the entire fruit?

May one peel many fruits and vegetables with intent to eat later on if he takes a bite from each fruit/vegetable right away?

Shabbos Workbook

Additional Notes

Shabbos Workbook

May one peel many fruits/vegetables for later on if he leaves the peels together with the fruits/vegetables?

May one peel right before the meal more fruits then needed for the purpose of making his guests feel comfortable in taking as much as they want, even though he knows that they will not eat all the fruits?

May one peel a fruit for a child to take with him upon leaving the house even though the child will not be eating it until later on?

May one peel fruits in order to make a fruit compute many hours prior to the meal in order so it extract and absorb taste into and from the salad?

May one remove a rotten/ wormy part of fruit/vegetable in order to eat the rest of the fruit/vegetable?

May one remove good fruits from amongst rotten ones to prevent them from rotting?

May one remove a worm or other bug from a fruit/vegetable?

Chapter 3: Miraked-Filtering wine, water and other liquids on Shabbos

1. Filtering liquids with a filter/strainer

Q&A

May one filter murky liquids which are not drinkable to majority of people for the purpose of washing dishes and the like?

216

Shabbos Workbook

Additional Notes

Shabbos Workbook

May one also today filter wine that has small twigs in it even though today such an occurrence is uncommon?

_____

_____

May one filter cork pieces out from wine on Shabbos?

_____

_____

May one who is particular to never drink unfiltered water filter it on Shabbos if it is drinkable by majority of people?

_____

_____

May a person which is not particular against drinking unfiltered water filter water for one who is particular in this and may thus not filter it?

_____

_____

May one who is particular to only drink filtered water, filter water for one who is not particular to do so?

_____

_____

May one use a Brita filter or a sink filter on Shabbos to filter water?

_____

_____

May one use the tab filter contained in all faucets on Shabbos or does this pose a filtering prohibition and thus one must remove it before Shabbos?

_____

_____

If the only available water is undrinkable, such as it has sand in it or worms and thus must be filtered, is there any way to do this on Shabbos?

_____

_____

May one pour a liquid which contains solids into the drain of the sink if the drain has a filter [as do most sink drains]?

_____

_____

Shabbos Workbook

May one use a spoon with holes to remove a solid out from a liquid, such as vegetables from soup?

Additional Notes

Shabbos Workbook

May one filter fruit pulp out from ones fruit drink?

May one filter baby cereal from their lumpy parts?

May one filter the fat out from milk?

May one use a salt shaker if there are pieces of hardened salt or rice inside?

Q&A regarding tea bags:

May one pour from a tea pot that has a strainer on its tip to prevent the leaves from falling in the cup?

May one use tea bags on Shabbos?

May one shake the tea bag while inside the liquid in order so more essence come out?

May one remove the tea bag from the tea?

May one pour the tea out from the cup, leaving the tea bag inside?

May one remove a sliced lemon from ones tea?

Shabbos Workbook

Additional Notes

Shabbos Workbook

May one use his hand to strain food for right away use?

_____

_____

2. Filtering liquids with a cloth:

_____

_____

Q&A

May one filter water with a cloth that is designated to be used for the purpose of filtering?

_____

_____

May one who is particular to never drink a certain unfiltered liquid filter it on Shabbos with a cloth?

_____

_____

Does the filtering, through cloth, of colored liquids contain the dyeing prohibition and if so then how does Admur here permit it?

_____

_____

May one filter murky liquids even with a cloth that is designated to be used for the purpose of filtering?

_____

_____

If the city water is undrinkable, such as it has sand in it or worms and thus must be filtered, is there any way to do this on Shabbos?

_____

_____

Does this restriction apply as well to non-murky liquids?

_____

_____

3. Filtering insects from water:

_____

_____

4. Filtering undrinkable liquids within the process of drinking:

_____

_____

Shabbos Workbook

<u>**Additional Notes**</u>

Shabbos Workbook

Q&A

Practically is only a "meticulous" person to avoid being lenient or every G-d fearing person?

Need one be stringent in this even when filtering water with a cloth that is designated to be used for the purpose of filtering?

Is there any difference in the above laws if the cloth is colored or white or if made of wool or linen?

May one who follows the lenient opinion filter even through a dirty cloth that is placed by ones mouth?

May one use ones shirt sleeve as a filter in this case?

May one who is stringent nevertheless filter colored liquid through cloth while drinking?

May one drink liquid that has solids mixed in it through a bottle that has a small hole in its top which blocks out the solids, such as by a baby bottle?

May one use a filtering straw on Shabbos to drink liquids which need filtering?

---

5. Filtering solid food parts which come from the same food:

Q&A on sifting:

May one sift flour on Shabbos?

Shabbos Workbook

Additional Notes

Shabbos Workbook

May one sift Matzah flour, baby formula and the like on Shabbos?

_____

_____

May one use a salt shaker if there are pieces of hardened salt or rice inside?

_____

_____

6. Shaking waste off from foods:

_____

_____

Q&A

May one use his hand to sift food for right away use by spreading the fingers slightly apart and pouring the mixture over the hand?

_____

_____

Shabbos Workbook

<u>Additional Notes</u>

Shabbos Workbook

The Laws of Zoreh/Winnowing:

1. Scattering items by throwing them into the wind
A. The prohibition

_____

_____

B. Spitting into the wind

_____

_____

C. Crumbling bread and throwing it into the wind:

_____

_____

Q&A

Does the Winnowing prohibition apply only if the wind will scatter the thrown item to many pieces or even if it simply carries the item, having it remain a single unit?

_____

_____

If the wind will not scatter the saliva but simply carry it along, is it nevertheless forbidden?

_____

_____

May one spit into the wind if having it carried in the wind is against his will, such as that he is spitting in a direction that the wind will throw the saliva back at him?

_____

_____

May one spit into the air if it is indefinite whether or not the wind will in truth take the saliva with it?

_____

_____

May one throw pieces of paper or other scatter-able materials into the wind?

_____

_____

May one spray a can into the air even though the content is being scattered or does this contain a Zoreh prohibition?

_____

_____

Shabbos Workbook

Additional Notes

Shabbos Workbook

The Laws of Mifareik -Squeezing liquids On Shabbos:

Chapter 1: The laws of squeezing juice from fruits/vegetables on Shabbos

1. The Biblical prohibition in Squeezing fruits on Shabbos:
A. Edible Fruits:

_____

_____

B. Inedible fruits:

_____

_____

2. The Rabbinical prohibition in squeezing fruits on Shabbos for the purpose of drinking their juice:
A. Strawberries, pomegranates and all fruits which are squeezed when there are plenty of them.

_____

_____

B. Edible fruits that are never squeezed for juice even when they have a lot of the fruit:

_____

_____

C. Fruits which are commonly squeezed but which their juices are not commonly drunk plain:

_____

_____

D. Squeezing out the juices of inedible fruits:

_____

_____

Q&A
If one is unsure whether a certain fruit is commonly squeezed to drink its juice, when there is plenty of that fruit available, is it still forbidden to squeeze it due to doubt?

_____

_____

If in ones city a fruit is not squeezed for its juice despite there being plentiful of it, may one squeeze the juice on Shabbos even if the rest of the world does squeeze it for juice?

_____

_____

Shabbos Workbook

Additional Notes

Shabbos Workbook

If a fruit is only squeezed for its juice within factories and then sold in ones city, while in ones private home they do not squeeze it for its juice even when there is plenty of it, is it nevertheless considered commonly squeezed and thus forbidden to squeeze on Shabbos or not?

_____

_____

Practically which fruits today are forbidden to squeeze?

_____

_____

May one use a juicer to squeeze fruits that are permitted to be squeezed?

_____

_____

May one use a spoon to eat out of a fruit that may not be squeezed to drink its juice, such as a grapefruit?

_____

_____

May one cut a fruit which may not be squeezed if in the process juice will get squeezed out, as is common with citric fruits?

_____

_____

May one cut a lemon over ones tea having its liquid fall into the tea?

_____

_____

May one squeeze out the juice of a fruit for no need at all but rather simply out of habit or the like?

_____

_____

If a food will only become edible due the squeezing may it nevertheless be squeezed?

_____

_____

3. Squeezing juice into food and liquid:
A. Squeezing Ripe Grapes into food [as opposed to liquid]:

_____

_____

B. Squeezing all other fruits which are edible in their raw state into foods:

_____

_____

Shabbos Workbook

<u>Additional Notes</u>

Shabbos Workbook

C. Squeezing fruits that are not fit to be eaten in their current state, into food:

_____

_____

D. Squeezing fruits into a liquid:

_____

_____

E. Squeezing into a creamy dip:

_____

_____

Q&A

May one squeeze fruits that are permitted to be squeezed using a juicer?

_____

_____

How much juice may one squeeze into a food?

_____

_____

May one squeeze juice onto sugar?

_____

_____

May one squeeze lemon into his food?

_____

_____

May one squeeze lemon onto sugar?

_____

_____

May one squeeze lemon into his tea on Shabbos?

_____

_____

May one cut a lemon over ones tea having its liquid fall into the tea?

Shabbos Workbook

Additional Notes

Shabbos Workbook

May one rub his hands on lemon in order to remove stains from his hands?

May one cut up a fruit salad despite the fact that juice will be squeezed in the process, and eventually eaten?

May one squeeze into food the juice of an inedible peel of an edible fruit, such as a lemon peel or orange peel?

If a food will only become edible due the squeezing may it nevertheless be squeezed?

May one squeeze juice into a food that also contains liquid, such as gravy or vegetable soup?

What is the definition of a liquid? How thin must the fluid be?

May one squeeze juice into a very liquidly dip, such as Italian dressing?

May one squeeze juice into a thick liquidly substance which is not meant for dips, such as fruit or vegetable puree?

May one squeeze juice into a melted fatty substance which will eventually congeal?

4. Squeezing in order to sweeten the fruit:

5. To suck the juice out from fruits:

236

Shabbos Workbook

Additional Notes

Shabbos Workbook

Q&A

May one who chooses to be stringent suck sugar cubes which have been dipped in tea or the like?

_____

_____

May one who is stringent suck a fruit/food when the entire food is already in his mouth?

_____

_____

May one suck out liquid that is absorbed in a cloth?

_____

_____

6. Juice which flowed on their own from fruits on Shabbos:
A. From grapes and olives:

_____

_____

B. From other fruits:

_____

_____

7. Squeezing juice out of pickles and other foods saturated with external liquids:
A. Squeezing out the liquid not for the sake of adding the liquid into food:

_____

_____

B. Squeezing cooked and pickled foods into food:

_____

_____

C. Squeezing out the food part of a fruit or cooked food

_____

_____

Q&A

Why does squeezing liquid out from a food not contain the Borer/separating prohibition?

_____

_____

If a food will only become edible due the squeezing may it nevertheless be squeezed?

_____

_____

Shabbos Workbook

Additional Notes

Shabbos Workbook

May one swipe up the gravy in his plate through pressing bread against the floor of the plate?

May juice which had been directly squeezed into a food be then squeezed out of that food?

When squeezing out liquid in order to enhance the food may one squeeze the liquid into a plate and then drink it?

May one squeeze out the juice of a fruit for no need at all but rather simply out of habit or the like?

Practically, may one squeeze out the oil from ones Sufganiya/ Latke?

May one squeeze out the oil from eggplant or vinegar from cucumber salad?

---

8. Pumping and squeezing milk on Shabbos

Q&A

May a woman pump milk to feed her baby if he refuses to suck from the breast?

May one squeeze the milk into the baby's mouth to stimulate it to eat?

May a woman use a pump to release milk in order to relieve breast pain?

Shabbos Workbook

Additional Notes

Shabbos Workbook

9. Sucking the milk from an animal

_____

_____

Chapter 2: Squeezing liquid from cloths on Shabbos

1. Squeezing cloths that have become wet

_____

_____

2. Spreading a cloth over an open bottle

_____

_____

3. Doing an action with a cloth which may cause liquid to squeeze out:
A. Inserting a wet cloth into the opening of a bottle

_____

_____

B. Using a sponge to clean

_____

_____

C. Plugging the hole of a barrel with a pipe and wet cloth on Shabbos

_____

_____

D. Plugging up the hole of a leaking pipe

_____

_____

Q&A

May one clean a dry table/counter using a wet cloth?

_____

_____

May one clean a wet counter or table [that does not contain an absorbent table cloth] using a dry cloth?

_____

_____

May one soak up a spill on Shabbos by placing on it a cloth napkin/tissue/rag?

_____

_____

Shabbos Workbook

May one wipe the liquid off a wet tablecloth using a knife and the like?

<u>Additional Notes</u>

Shabbos Workbook

The Laws of Nolad- Melting and freezing snow, ice, gravy, soap, and fat:

1. Crushing and breaking ice/snow with one's body:
A. Crushing a piece of snow or ice with ones hands:

_____

_____

B. Washing with icy water/Crushing ice in a way that it melts directly into water

_____

_____

C. Breaking ice in order to get to the water which is underneath it

_____

_____

D. Breaking a piece off from ice

_____

_____

E. Urinating on snow

_____

_____

F. Stepping on snow

_____

_____

Q&A

May one crush a piece of ice that is in ones cup of water or juice?

_____

_____

May one break the surface of ice that covers over drinks that have begun to freeze?

_____

_____

May one break the pieces of ice from ones ice tray in order to place it in his drink?

_____

_____

Shabbos Workbook

May one break the surface of ice that is over a very large barrel?

Additional Notes

Shabbos Workbook

May an item which has frozen onto ones window sill or other area attached to ones house be removed?

_____

_____

May one remove the sheets of ice that have frozen on ones windows?

_____

_____

May one melt ice if the resultant water will anyways go to waste, such as to throw ice cubes in ones sink?

_____

_____

May one pour water onto ice/salt/sugar and other dissolvable items?

_____

_____

Is snow Muktzah?

_____

_____

May one sweep snow or ice away from his lawn?

_____

_____

May one make or throw snow balls?

_____

_____

May one spread salt on snow?

_____

_____

2. Placing ice into a glass of liquid:

_____

_____

Q&A

May one pour the liquid onto the ice in ones cup?

_____

_____

Shabbos Workbook

Additional Notes

Shabbos Workbook

May one pour some water onto an ice tray to help break the ice?

May one pour water onto salt/sugar and other dissolvable items?

May one mix the ice cube in his drink using a spoon or the like?

May one place a dissolvable item such as sugar and instant coffee into liquid and then mix it with a spoon so it dissolves?

May one place soap into a cup of liquid and have it dissolve and then use that to wash ones hands?

3. Placing a frozen/congealed item in an area where it will melt on its own:
A. Placing congealed fat in an area where it will melt:

B. Placing plain ice in an area where it will melt on its own

Q&A
May one melt congealed chicken, meat or fish gravy near a flame or in the sun?

May one melt ice cream on Shabbos?

May one melt a frozen baby bottle in the sun or near heat in an area that it will not reach Yad Soledes?

Shabbos Workbook

Additional Notes

Shabbos Workbook

May one place ice cubes on top of bottles of soda and the like in order to cool them down?

May one throw out his leftover ice cubes into the kitchen sink despite the fact that they will melt here?

May one place ice cubes in his cup with the intent of having it melt and then drinking its water?

May one defrost frozen foods/liquids on Shabbos, such as defrosting a frozen bottle of soda?

May one place ice cubes in a serving tray for the meal despite the fact that they will melt?

4. Washing ones hands with salt/ soap/fats

Q&A

Does washing ones hands with a bar of soap contain the smoothening prohibition [Mimacheik] and would thus be prohibited according to all?

Is washing ones hands with a bar of soap which contain lettering contain the "erasing" prohibition?

May one place soap into a cup of liquid and have it dissolve and then use that to wash ones hands?

May one wash his hands with scented soaps?

Shabbos Workbook

Additional Notes

Shabbos Workbook

May one place a bar of scented soap into his toilet?

Supplement: Freezing foods/liquid on Shabbos
May one make seltzer water on Shabbos?

Q&A on Freezing foods/liquid on Shabbos:
May one make ice cubes, or freeze drinks on Shabbos?

May one merely place a bottle in the freezer so it becomes cold as opposed to freeze?

May one place liquids in the freezer before Shabbos having them freeze over Shabbos?

May one place solid foods in the freezer on Shabbos?

May one freeze a liquidly food in order so it not spoil?

May one enter foods with gravy into the fridge/freezer despite that they will congeal?

May one freeze ice cream on Shabbos?

May one melt ice cream on Shabbos?

Shabbos Workbook

Additional Notes

Shabbos Workbook

The Laws of Molid Reiach:

1. Molid Reiach-The laws of placing perfume and the like onto objects/clothing and one's skin:
A. Smoking fruits on Yom Tov over incense:

_____

_____

B. Absorbing a good smell into a cloth :

_____

_____

C. Placing scents into liquids and washing hands with scented liquids

_____

_____

D. Removing mouth odor:

_____

_____

Q&A

May one spray perfume or cologne onto his/her body or clothing on Shabbos?

_____

_____

May one apply deodorant on Shabbos:

_____

_____

May one wash his hands with scented soaps?

_____

_____

May one use scented oil in cases in which it is allowed to smear it on Shabbos [as explained in "The Laws of oiling Skin"]?

_____

_____

May one spray air freshener in his room or bathroom?

_____

_____

Shabbos Workbook

May one use a toilet that contains scented toilet soap?

May one use mouthwash to remove bad odor:

May one place a good smelling powder or spray on his feet?

Additional Notes

Shabbos Workbook

The Prohibition of Dyeing:

1. The Prohibition of dyeing clothing and other objects

_____

_____

2. Dyeing foods

_____

_____

Q&A

May one on Shabbos place food coloring into foods or liquids that are planned to be sold?

_____

_____

May one dye water or other liquids?

_____

_____

3. Wiping stained hands on a cloth:

_____

_____

Q&A

May one who wet his hands with wine use a towel or non-disposable napkin to dry them?

_____

_____

May one use a tissue or disposable napkin to wipe his stained hands?

_____

_____

May one filter red wine through a cloth?

_____

_____

4. Treating a bleeding wound on Shabbos:

_____

_____

Shabbos Workbook

Q&A

May a bandage be used over a bleeding wound?

May one place a tissue or disposable napkin on the wound?

May one wrap a towel over a bleeding wound?

One who has cleaned a wound from blood, may he place on it a cloth even though he knows that it will eventually continue to bleed?

---

5. Dyeing ones skin with pigment/Applying makeup:

Q&A

May a woman apply nail polish or lip stick on Shabbos?

May a woman apply face powder ["foundation"] to her face on Shabbos?

May one apply cream to their face on Shabbos?

May one smear Dead sea mud on their face on Shabbos?

May one remove nail polish on Shabbos?

Shabbos Workbook

May one take a suntan on Shabbos?

_____

_____

6. Making dye on Shabbos:

_____

_____

General Q&A

May one use Q-tips on Shabbos?

_____

_____

Shabbos Workbook

Additional Notes

Shabbos Workbook

The laws of Tanning skins; and Salting foods on Shabbos:

1. The Biblical prohibition- Tanning and salting skins:

_____

_____

2. The Rabbinical prohibition- Salting foods:
A. Salting raw meat [which is edible by some in its raw state] in order to soften in

_____

_____

B. Salting in order to preserve/ pickling foods

_____

_____

C. Salting foods which salt helps to change their natural state

_____

_____

D. Salting foods which salt only helps to give taste

_____

_____

Q&A

May one place food in vinegar on Shabbos?

_____

May one make salt water in order to soak in it cut cucumbers which will be served for the Shabbos meal?

_____

May one place sugar on fruits or vegetables without restriction?

_____

_____

May one sugar his grapefruit on Shabbos?

_____

_____

May one place pepper on foods without restriction?

_____

_____

Shabbos Workbook

Additional Notes

Shabbos Workbook

May one salt more than one bean at a time and the like of other foods which are usually eaten many at one time?

_____

_____

If the reason behind the prohibition to salt more than one food at a time is due to that it appears like pickling which itself is prohibited according to some due to that it appears like cooking, why may one therefore not be lenient to salt already cooked foods, after all there is no cooking after cooking?

_____

_____

Is the placing of oil and salt in ones food only allowed to be done in proximity to the upcoming meal?

_____

_____

Is there any reason to be stringent to first place in the oil and then the salt?

_____

_____

May one also be lenient like the second opinion, or must one be stringent like both opinions?

_____

_____

May one salt more than one food at a time if he plans to eat both of them at the same time?

_____

_____

May one be lenient to salt many foods and then add oil to it immediately even according to the first opinion, and if not then should one today practically be lenient in the above?

_____

_____

If one salted a food that salt helps change their natural state on Shabbos without adding oil/vinegar to it may one still eat it on Shabbos?

_____

_____

May one salt his food even much time prior to beginning the upcoming meal?

_____

_____

Are tomatoes considered foods which salt only helps to give taste?

_____

_____

Shabbos Workbook

Additional Notes

Shabbos Workbook

May one place vinegar into his cucumber salad on Shabbos?

_____

_____

May one add salt to his vegetable salad prior to the meal?

_____

_____

May one add salt to his cooked meat or chulent?

_____

_____

May one add salt to a tomato salad?

_____

_____

3. Making salt water on Shabbos:
A. For pickling foods:

_____

_____

B. For dipping foods into:

_____

_____

Q&A
According to Admur may one salt his food even much time prior to beginning the upcoming meal?

_____

_____

May one make salt water in order to soak in it cut cucumbers which will be served for the Shabbos meal?

_____

_____

May one make sugar water on Shabbos with two thirds being sugar?

_____

_____

Shabbos Workbook

<u>Additional Notes</u>

Shabbos Workbook

The laws of Crushing, grinding, mashing, and Cutting foods on Shabbos:

1. Grinding foods:
A. Crushing spices

B. Grinding foods that do not grow from the ground:

C. Grinding foods that grow from the ground

D. Grinding food with ones teeth for later use

Q&A

May one crumble a lump of salt or other spice with his hands?

May one crumble a thick piece of snuff with his hands in order to smell it?

May one crumble a piece of a spice with his hands in order to smell it?

What is the law with regards to grinding sugar cubes?

May one grind foods that do not grow on the ground, or foods that have already been ground such as bread, without any restriction?

Shabbos Workbook

Additional Notes

Shabbos Workbook

Examples of utensils which are designated for grinding and thus may never be used on Shabbos:

_____

_____

May one grind without restriction foods which grow from the earth which are not commonly ground?

_____

_____

May one grind foods which are already very small?

_____

_____

May one grind bread/crackers/Matzah and other foods of the like which have been ground in their process of preparation?

_____

_____

May one mash foods on Shabbos?

_____

_____

May one mash any food using a fork or spoon? /Is mashing with a spoon/fork considered an irregularity?

_____

_____

When mashing a food in the permitted ways must one do so directly prior to the meal?

_____

_____

May one mash and spread banana or avocado on bread using the teeth of a fork?

_____

_____

May one mash cooked fruits and vegetables using the teeth of a knife?

_____

_____

May one mash eggs/meat/chicken using the teeth of a fork?

_____

_____

Shabbos Workbook

Additional Notes

Shabbos Workbook

2. Cutting foods to small pieces:
A. To cut spices with a knife

B. Cutting to small pieces foods that do not grow from the ground

C. Cutting to small pieces foods that grow from the ground

D. What items may be used to cut with? May graters and the like be used?

E. Cutting non food items to very small pieces

Q&A

May one cut fresh jalapeño peppers to small pieces in order to eat right away?

Is a cinnamon stick considered a spice or a food?

May one grate horse radish, or cut it very small?

Are onions and garlic considered spices?

May one cut sugar cubes to small pieces [I.E. Is sugar considered a spice?

Shabbos Workbook

<u>Additional Notes</u>

Shabbos Workbook

When cutting the food slightly large may one do so even much time prior to the meal?

What is the definition of cutting small?

May one cut a fruit/vegetable to very thin slices [long but thin]?

If one transgressed and cut fruits/vegetables into small pieces much time prior to the meal, may the food still be eaten?

May one use an egg slicer on Shabbos to cut eggs?

May one use a knife which is specifically made for cutting small?

May one use a bread machine to slice bread on Shabbos?

Shabbos Workbook

Additional Notes

Shabbos Workbook

The laws of Kneading:

1. The definition of kneading-Placing liquid in a food or mixing it in?

_____

_____

Q&A

May one place the knead-able food into the liquid [as opposed to liquid into food] even according to the second opinion?

_____

_____

Does the kneading prohibition also apply when adding liquids other than water into a mixture?

_____

May one knead food right before a meal, as is allowed with Borer and cutting small?

_____

May one mix a foods own liquids into that food?

_____

What form of mixtures are defined as kneading?

_____

May one mix two liquids into each other?

_____

Does kneading a single food without any liquid contain a kneading prohibition?

_____

May one place sesame seeds/almonds and the like into honey on Shabbos?

_____

_____

May one knead on Yom Tov?

_____

_____

Shabbos Workbook

Additional Notes

Shabbos Workbook

2. The Mixtures that are not allowed to be kneaded:
A. First opinion

_____

_____

B. The second opinion

_____

_____

C. The Final Ruling

_____

_____

Q&A

Are we also stringent like the first opinion in cases that only according to them kneading is forbidden?

_____

_____

When permitted to be kneaded, must one do so right before the meal?

_____

_____

What is the definition of a thin mixture?

_____

_____

When making a thin mixture must one place all the liquid into the food simultaneously or may one place it in a little at a time?

_____

_____

If mixing liquid into a food before Shabbos will ruin that food is there room to be lenient like the first opinion to make it into a thick mixture on Shabbos?

_____

_____

If one forgot to knead a food before Shabbos may he be lenient like the first opinion mentioned to make a thick mixture using an irregularity?

_____

_____

When making a drink using dissolvable powders must one do so with an irregularity?

_____

Shabbos Workbook

Additional Notes

Shabbos Workbook

If the adding of liquid to a certain food will at first thicken it and only after some mixing thin it out, may one make it into a thin mixture on Shabbos?

---

3. The definition of an "irregularity"

Q&A

What does one do if he does not know in what way a certain mixture is mixed?

If one is unable to mix the mixture together using his fingers or bowl may he use a spoon?

May one mix the mixture quickly when using his hands to mix as is required?

---

4. May one knead a food which was already kneaded?

Q&A

If one placed water in the batter before Shabbos, may one knead it or add more water to it on Shabbos?

How much liquid must be added to a food before Shabbos to consider it previously kneaded?

May one add liquid on Shabbos to a mixture which was previously kneaded only with its own liquids?

May one add more solid into a mixture that was kneaded before Shabbos in order to thicken it?

Shabbos Workbook

Additional Notes

Shabbos Workbook

May one add liquid to ones dip [which was kneaded with liquid before Shabbos] if it is now dry?

May one knead an already kneaded item that has now become a solid, such as bread/crackers and the like?

May one dip a piece of bread in soup or a biscuit in tea/coffee?

May one break his bread/biscuits into pieces and place them into his soup/tea?

May one add liquid to a cooked dish on Shabbos if doing so will make it into a thick mixture?

5. How to make Charoses on Yom Tov which falls on Shabbos

6. Kneading course flour for animal fodder:

Practical Q&A

May one make instant foods through mixing water and a powder together, such as instant mashed potatoes/oatmeal/porridge/rice/pudding?

When making a bottle for an infant from milk powder must it be made with the required irregularities?

When adding liquid into cocoa powder and the like must one do so with an irregularity?

Shabbos Workbook

Additional Notes

Shabbos Workbook

May one make Techina on Shabbos?

May one make oatmeal on Shabbos?

May one mix mayonnaise/oil/honey into cut fruits/vegetables and foods of the like?

May one make an egg salad with mayonnaise on Shabbos?

May one mix mayonnaise into tuna fish on Shabbos?

Does mashing a banana and the like contain a kneading prohibition?

May one knead liquid into a mashed banana?

May one mix a batch of lemon aid or other juice very quickly with a spoon?

May one mix sugar with cocoa powder?

May one mix the peanut butter oil into the peanut butter on Shabbos?

May one add soup to his rice/lentils/chulent if doing so will make it into a thick mixture?

Shabbos Workbook

Additional Notes

Shabbos Workbook

May one combine honey with cream cheese?

May one combine two different yogurts, or yogurt with soft cheese?

May one break biscuits into his yogurt?

May one add sugar to soft cheese or yogurt?

May one combine cocoa powder with butter or margarine?

May one pour liquid onto loose earth?/May one urinate on the earth?

May one spit into a vessel or area which contains sand/dirt?

May one urinate onto mud?

May one cover liquid [such as urine] with sand/dirt?

Shabbos Workbook

Additional Notes

Shabbos Workbook

Shulchan Aruch Chapter 322:

1. An egg laid on Shabbos:

2. Fruits which fell off a tree:

Q&A
Are vegetables which have become detached from the ground on Shabbos forbidden?

Tikkun Keli by foods:

Shulchan Aruch Chapter 323:

1. Buying items on credit on Shabbos:

2. Borrowing items on Shabbos:

3. Measuring on Shabbos:

4. Transporting items from one area to another on Shabbos:

5. Washing dishes on Shabbos:

Shabbos Workbook

Additional Notes

Shabbos Workbook

Q&A On washing Dishes

May one wash dirty dishes even if he has more clean dishes available?

_____

_____

May one wash the dishes after his last meal if they are tarnishing the cleanliness of the house?

_____

_____

May one wash dishes on Shabbos if he will only be using them the next Shabbos?

_____

_____

May one soak the dishes in water after his last Shabbos meal?

_____

_____

May one wash his food pots on Shabbos?

_____

_____

May one enter water into his food pot in order to let the pot soak?

_____

_____

May one wash his Kiddush cup out after Kiddush of the day meal?

_____

_____

Q&A on Soaps

Which soaps may be used to wash dishes?

_____

_____

May one place soap into a cup of liquid and have it dissolve and then use that to wash dishes?

_____

_____

Q&A on Sponges

Which forms of sponges may be used to wash the dishes?

_____

_____

Shabbos Workbook

Q&A on Polishing

May one polish glass dishes?

_____

_____

May one polish silverware, copperware and other silver vessels?

_____

_____

May one remove rust from metal, such as from the blades of a knife?

_____

_____

5. Immersing vessels in a Mikveh:

_____

_____

Q&A

May one immerse a vessel on Shabbos if there is a doubt as to whether it even requires immersion?

_____

_____

6. Issur which fell into one's food on Shabbos:

_____

_____

<u>Additional Notes</u>

Shabbos Workbook

Shulchan Aruch Chapter 324:

Feeding animals on Shabbos

1. Feeding animals:

_____

_____

Q&A

May one feed someone else's animal?

_____

_____

May one throw away leftovers in an area that animals will be able to eat them?

_____

_____

May one feed a hungry wild animal from outside?

_____

_____

May one chase an animal outside if it has food in his mouth?

_____

_____

2. Preparing food for one's animals:

_____

_____

Q&A

May one do Borer for the sake of one's animal?

_____

_____

3. Gavage: Force-feeding animals that are dependent on oneself for food:

_____

_____

4. Allowing one's animal to graze:

_____

_____

Shabbos Workbook

5. Giving an animal other animals' leftovers:

Kneading course flour for animals on Shabbos:
A. First Opinion:

B. Second Opinion:

C. Final Ruling

Cutting meat for a dog:

Additional Notes

Shabbos Workbook

Chapter 325: A gentile which did forbidden work for a Jew:

Giving food and other items to a gentile on Shabbos:

Inviting him for the meal:

Giving him food to carry into a public domain:

Giving objects to a Gentile on Shabbos:

Returning a collateral to a gentile on Shabbos

Exceptions to all the above restrictions:

Giving back collateral of clothing:

Benefiting from items which a gentile did labor to on Shabbos for his own behalf

Taking Bakery bread from a gentile baker on Shabbos:

Food cooked by a gentile on Shabbos which is not Bishul Akum

Juices squeezed by a gentile on Shabbos:

Shabbos Workbook

Additional Notes

Shabbos Workbook

Fruits picked by a gentile on Shabbos:

Items carried from a private domain to a public domain on behalf of gentiles:

Definition of an action done for a gentile's behalf:

The general rule of an acquaintance of a gentile:

Coffins and graves prepared by gentiles on Shabbos on behalf of gentiles:

Q&A
Are other actions which occurred on their own on Shabbos also forbidden to be benefited from?

Benefiting from items which a gentile did labor to on Shabbos for a Jews behalf

The law regarding the person for whom the work was done:

The Reason for why it is forbidden until the above amount of time passes after Shabbos

The law regarding others:

The definition of "Kdei Sheyasu":

Shabbos Workbook

Additional Notes

Shabbos Workbook

The law in a case of doubt in whether or not the item had work done on Shabbos for a Jews behalf:

The reason:

Other Opinions:

The Final Ruling

The law by a case that the gentile brought over fruits as a present or to sell:

Trapped creatures:

Items which were brought on Shabbos from past the city limit

Brought for a gentile

Brought for a Jew:

The reason:

Moving the food:

Shabbos Workbook

Additional Notes

Shabbos Workbook

Not to carry the food past a four cubit radius:

_____

_____

Items brought by ship:

_____

_____

Those that the food was brought on their behalf may not switch the packages

The definition of waiting "Kdie Sheyasu" after Shabbos when brought from outside the Techum

_____

_____

If one knows from where the food was brought:

_____

_____

If one does not now from where the food was brought:

_____

_____

Other Opinions

_____

_____

Their reasoning is:

_____

_____

The Final Ruling:

_____

_____

By other scenarios of "Kdei Sheyasu" one may wait from the night after Shabbos:

_____

_____

Food which is questionable as to whether or not was brought from outside the city limits:

_____

_____

Shabbos Workbook

Additional Notes

Shabbos Workbook

The reason for this stringency despite it being a case of doubt in a Rabbinical prohibition is:

_____

_____

Other Opinions

_____

_____

Final Ruling:

_____

_____

Food that was brought by a gentile that lives within ones city:

_____

_____

If he also has one house outside the city limit:

_____

_____

If he has two houses outside the city limit:

_____

_____

Other cases of works of a gentile done on Shabbos

Water filled by a gentile and carried from a private to public domain:

_____

_____

On behalf of a gentile:

_____

_____

The reason for this is:

_____

_____

If the gentile is an acquaintance of the Jew:

_____

_____

Shabbos Workbook

Additional Notes

Shabbos Workbook

On behalf of a Jew:

_____

_____

The reason for this is

_____

_____

From or into a Karmalis:

_____

_____

The custom today: Asking a gentile to bring items from a Karmalis on Shabbos:

_____

_____

The reason:

_____

_____

Restrictions to the above allowance:

_____

_____

If a gentile picked grass for his own behalf:

_____

_____

If the gentile is an acquaintance of the Jew:

_____

_____

The rule by Jewish acquaintances of a gentile who did work for himself:

_____

_____

Suspicion of increased work:

_____

_____

No suspicion of increased work:

_____

_____

Shabbos Workbook

Additional Notes

Shabbos Workbook

Work done which is evident that it was done for a Jew

Allowing a gentile to feed herbs to ones animal if the gentile picked the herbs for that purpose:

The reason why one does not have to protest the picking of the grass:

If the grass belongs to the Jew:

The reason why one need not protest letting his animal eat it

Coffins and graves prepared by gentiles on Shabbos:

On behalf of gentiles:

On behalf of Jews:

Made in a public area on behalf of a Jew:

Other actions done in public:

Other Opinions

Shabbos Workbook

Additional Notes

Shabbos Workbook

The Final Ruling:

_____

_____

If one hired the gentile to do the work for him

_____

_____

A eulogy cymbal that was brought to a Jew on Shabbos through a public domain:

_____

_____

Brought from an actual public domain:

_____

_____

Brought in a publicized manner:

_____

_____

Brought from a Karmalis:

_____

_____

The reason for this leniency is:

_____

_____

If there is doubt from where it was brought:

_____

_____

Shabbos Workbook

Supplement Chapter 226 Halacha 13

A bathhouse which was heated on Shabbos by a gentile:

_____

_____

Majority gentile population:

_____

_____

Majority Jewish population:

_____

_____

Half-Half:

_____

_____

Additional Notes

Shabbos Workbook

The Laws of Bathing, Showering, and Swimming on Shabbos:

1. The prohibition of bathing/showering on Shabbos in hot water:
A. Bathing in hot water heated through fire:

_____

_____

B. Showering in hot water heated through fire:

_____

_____

C. Bathing in hot water heated through fire one limb at a time or minority of one's body:

_____

_____

D. Bathing in water that was not heated through fire:

_____

_____

E. May one bathe in warm water?

_____

_____

Q&A
If one placed cold water onto his blech right before Shabbos, and it was thus only heated on Shabbos, may one bathe minority of his limbs in such water?

_____

_____

If one mixed hot water that was heated from before Shabbos with cold water [in a way permitted to be done, such as cold pouring water into a Keli Sheiyni], may one bathe minority of his body with this water on Shabbos?

_____

_____

May one bathe in water that was heated by sun, such as in ones solar boiler?

_____

_____

What is defined as warm water as opposed to hot water?

_____

_____

Shabbos Workbook

Additional Notes

Shabbos Workbook

2. Bathing/Showering with cold water; Washing hands in a river; Walking in the rain:
A. The law and custom:

_____

_____

B. Halachic matters which need to be followed when bathing in a river:

_____

_____

C. Washing ones hands in a river:

_____

_____

D. Walking outside while it is raining:

_____

_____

Q&A

If one for whatever reason entered a river or sea on Shabbos may he walk to shore with the drops of water on him and then dry himself on the shore, or must he dry himself as soon as he lifts his body above water?

_____

_____

May one walk 4 cubits in a public domain if there are still drops of water in ones beard?

_____

_____

According to today's custom may one nevertheless bathe part of his body in cold water?

_____

_____

According to today's custom may one nevertheless immerse in a Mikveh on Shabbos?

_____

_____

May one who has just awoken from sleep pour cold water on his head to revive himself?

_____

_____

May one take a cold shower on a very hot day?

_____

_____

Shabbos Workbook

Additional Notes

Shabbos Workbook

May one walk outside while it is snowing even though he will inevitably carry the snow?

---

3. Bathing for healing purposes:

Q&A

May a person who is in pain bathe in hot water heated before Shabbos?

May one who showers daily and avoiding so on Shabbos will cause him extreme discomfort shower with hot water heated from before Shabbos?

May one today bathe in Tiberius springs for healing purposes?

According to today's custom to not bathe at all on Shabbos may one nevertheless immerse in a Mikveh on Shabbos?

How many times is one to immerse in the Mikveh on Shabbos day?

May one who desires to immerse in a Mikveh do so today even in a river or sea?

May one immerse in a hot Mikveh on Shabbos?

May one swim in a Mikveh on Shabbos?

Shabbos Workbook

Additional Notes

Shabbos Workbook

May one splash away the dirt that floats on the surface of a Mikvah?

___

May one remove the stopper which attaches the Mikveh to the pit of rain water?

___

4. The allowance to dry oneself with a towel on Shabbos:

___

5. The prohibition of squeezing liquid from hair on Shabbos:

___

Q&A

What areas of hair contain the squeezing prohibition?

___

May one wash one's beard/head and the like on Shabbos?

___

May one pad his head or beard with a towel in order so it absorbs the water?

___

May one leave a towel over his wet hair letting the water get absorbed into the towel on its own?

___

May one squeeze the water out from his eyelids after leaving the Mikveh?

___

May one scratch his hair when it is wet?

___

Shabbos Workbook

Additional Notes

Shabbos Workbook

If while drinking one got his mustache filled with water, may he squeeze the water out?

_____

_____

6. Swimming on Shabbos:

_____

_____

Q&A

What is the definition of swimming?

_____

_____

May one enter into a non –rimmed pool if he will not swim in it?

_____

_____

What is defined as a rim for the pool/What is the law if a pool is not filled to the top?

_____

_____

If a rimmed pool is in a public area may one swim in it in cases that one is allowed to bathe in cold water?

_____

_____

May one who entered a pool to immerse in, or to cool off in, swim in that pool?

_____

_____

May one swim or tread inside a Mikveh?

_____

_____

7. Splashing twigs away while in a body of water:

_____

_____

Q&A

May one splash away the dirt that floats on the surface of a Mikvah?

_____

_____

Shabbos Workbook

Additional Notes

Shabbos Workbook

May one use a net to remove dirt from a Mikveh on Shabbos?

---

8. Perspiring on Shabbos in a bathhouse:

May one enter a Mikveh in which he knows that its heat will cause him to perspire?

May one take a suntan on Shabbos?

---

9. Warming up ones wet body near a fire:

---

10. Treating stomach pains with a vessel of hot water

Q&A
If the water is placed in a closed bottle may one place it on his stomach?

---

11. Washing oneself with liquid that also contains hair removal liquid on Shabbos:

---

12. Washing ones hands in salt or soap:

Q&A
Does washing ones hands with a bar of soap contain the smoothening prohibition [Mimachek] and would thus be prohibited according to all?

318

Shabbos Workbook

Additional Notes

Shabbos Workbook

Is washing ones hands with a bar of soap which contain lettering contain the "erasing" prohibition?

May one place soap into a cup of liquid and have it dissolve and then use that to wash ones hands?

May one wash his hands with liquid soap?

May one wash his hands with scented soaps?

May one place a bar of scented soap into his toilet?

---

13. May one use a bath sponge to rub against his skin on Shabbos?

Q&A

May one rub himself with a dry sponge designated for Shabbos if his body is wet?

May one scrub himself with a wet sponge made of synthetic hairs?

May one wash his body using a glove?

---

14. Bathing after Shabbos in water that was heated on Shabbos
A. The water of a bathhouse that got heated on its own on Shabbos:

Shabbos Workbook

B. A bathhouse which was heated on Shabbos by a gentile:

_____

_____

Q&A

If the water was heated by a Jew on Shabbos what is the law?

_____

_____

If one goes to a country club which heats their water on Shabbos may one use bathe in that water after Shabbos?

_____

Additional Notes

Shabbos Workbook

The Laws of oiling one's skin, and oiling leather on Shabbos:

1. Giving an oil massage for pleasure purposes on Shabbos:

_____

_____

Q&A

May one use scented oil in the above cases in which it is allowed to smear it on Shabbos?

_____

May one smear thick oil on one's body?

_____

May one take a suntan on Shabbos?

_____

_____

2. Smearing oil for medical treatment:
A. Applying oil mixtures for treatment:

_____

B. Applying plain oil for treatment:

_____

C. Applying oil or an oil mixture near the wound, having it flow onto it:

_____

Q&A

In our provinces is oil considered something that is only smeared for healing purposes?

_____

May one smear oil on cracked or dry skin, such as chapped lips?

_____

Shabbos Workbook

Additional Notes

Shabbos Workbook

May one smear oil on a baby for healing purposes [such as he has a rash and the like]?

_____

_____

May one smear oil over itchy skin [however the skin is not cracked or dry]?

_____

_____

3. Oiling leather on Shabbos:

_____

_____

4. Softening and hardening leather on Shabbos:

_____

_____

Q&A

May one stretch out his leather shoes on Shabbos if they are cutting into his skin?

_____

_____

May one enter shoetrees into his shoes on Shabbos to upkeep the shoes?

_____

_____

Shabbos Workbook

Additional Notes

Shabbos Workbook

The Laws of Taking Medicine, Treating the sick, and applying first Aid:

Chapter 1: The laws of one whose life is in danger:

1. The Obligation to help save someone's life even if it involves doing Shabbos transgressions:
A. The Mitzvah and its reason:

_____

_____

B. Helping to save a life even he will further live only momentarily

_____

_____

C. Being swift to transgress Shabbos to save a life even if doing so swiftly involves additional transgressions

_____

_____

D. One who refuses to accept treatment?

_____

_____

E. May a treatment be started on Shabbos if the doctors say that he will regardless live until after Shabbos?

_____

_____

F. If many dates were picked when only one was needed

_____

_____

G. Must one help save another Jew if there is danger involved for him

_____

_____

H. Saving a Jewish robber from death on Shabbos

_____

_____

I. Transgressing Shabbos to help save a person which is questionably Jewish

_____

_____

Shabbos Workbook

Additional Notes

Shabbos Workbook

J. Checking if the person is already dead

Q&A

May one desecrate Shabbos to help save one who is committing suicide?

May one desecrate Shabbos to save a Jew which does not keep Shabbos, or a heretic?

Practically today may one give medical treatment to a gentile on Shabbos, and may he desecrate Shabbos on his behalf?

May one turn on a resuscitation machine to help revive one who is not breathing?

---

2. Who should do the desecration of Shabbos for the ill person- Jew/Gentile/Man/Woman/Child?
A. First Opinion

B. Other Opinions

C. The Final Ruling:

Q&A

Should a gentile doctor be given to take care of the treatment over a Jewish doctor?

Should a religious doctor be given to take care of the treatment over a non-religious Jewish doctor?

Shabbos Workbook

Additional Notes

Shabbos Workbook

May woman nurses be initially entrusted with care for the patient or is one to request specifically a man?

_____

_____

3. Which treatments may be done?
A. Must use a known treatment or one prescribed by a medical expert

_____

_____

B. Must a treatment that does not involve Shabbos desecration be given over one that does

_____

_____

C. Must one do the Biblical prohibitions involved in the treatment with an irregularity

_____

_____

D. May non-urgent actions be done?

_____

_____

E. An example of the above dispute in D-Lighting a bonfire for a lethally ill person over warming him with clothes:

_____

_____

F. May a kosher animal be slaughtered if there is non-kosher meat readily available?

_____

_____

Q&A

What's Halachicly better, to drive to the hospital oneself or to call an ambulance?

_____

_____

Matters to be aware of when driving to the hospital:

_____

_____

If a light needs to be turned on and one has different options of which light to use is there preference of one type of light over another?

_____

_____

Shabbos Workbook

Additional Notes

Shabbos Workbook

Should one ask a neighbor to drive the patient to the hospital rather then call an ambulance?

Must one drive his sick neighbor to the hospital in order to prevent an ambulance from being called?

If one needs hot food and the like must he ask his neighbor for it rather then make it himself through doing a prohibition?

Must one provide his Shabbos food for his sick neighbor in order to prevent them from needing to cook food on Shabbos?

In cases that an action may only be done with an irregularity, what is defined to be an irregularity?

Is doing an action with two people if it is normally done alone considered an irregularity?

How may one dial the telephone with an irregularity?

May the deathly ill's relatives be alerted to come visit him?

May a relative or friend accompany the patient to the hospital?

May a Tzaddik or Torah Scholar be alerted to pray for the patient if doing so involves prohibitions?

Shabbos Workbook

Additional Notes

Shabbos Workbook

May a doctor/ EMT which drove a patient to the hospital return home on Shabbos?

May one who was released from a hospital on Shabbos return home on Shabbos?

May one salt the meat to remove its blood?

Is there a Halachic difference between slaughtering a cow and a chicken if both are available?

4. Cases that are defined as life threatening situations:
A. A wound in an inner limb is assumed to be deadly unless known otherwise:

B. A wound on an outer limb-Some require evaluation

C. A wound on the back of the hand or feet

D. A wound from iron:

E. Blisters by the rectum

F. Furuncle

Shabbos Workbook

Additional Notes

Shabbos Workbook

G. Fever accompanied with shivering

_____

_____

H. Swallowed a leech

_____

_____

I. Bitten by rabid dog or other deadly creature

_____

_____

J. Treating blood accumulation

_____

_____

K .Eye Pain

_____

_____

L. A baby which has gotten locked in a room:

_____

_____

M. A sinking ship; drowning person; a Jew being chased by a gentile

_____

_____

N. Extinguishing a lethal fire

_____

_____

O. Fighting Robbers/Enemy Soldiers

_____

_____

P. Murderers

_____

_____

Q. Saving a Jew from forcibly giving up his religion

_____

_____

Shabbos Workbook

Additional Notes

Shabbos Workbook

R. If there are many doubts involved in the case

S. Extinguishing candle for ill which need sleep

T. Extinguishing candle due to fear of bandits

Q&A

May one desecrate Shabbos for the above mentioned symptoms defined as life threatening even today when modern medicine has diminished the severity of these symptoms?

May one desecrate Shabbos for even a mere cut due to a metal knife?

May one desecrate Shabbos if he was hit by a metal or wooden item and no blood came out but a bruise was formed?

May one desecrate Shabbos to search for a lost child?

May one contact the police or the relatives in a case of a lost child which one has found?

If the robber is simply coming for the money, must the owner comply with his commands, such as giving him the key to the safe if he is asked for it, or may he fight back and desecrate Shabbos?

May one fight off the robber to prevent his money from getting stolen if he knows the robber does not intend to harm him?

Shabbos Workbook

Additional Notes

Shabbos Workbook

May one call the police if he sees a robber entering another person's house?

_____

_____

May one call the police if he sees robbers entering into a bank or the like?

_____

_____

A list of different symptoms which are to be considered life threatening:

_____

_____

5. Illnesses which require a Doctors evaluation
A. All Doctors which did the evaluation agree that is dangerous:

_____

_____

B. What to do in a case of split of opinion amongst two doctors:

_____

_____

C. A split opinion between the doctor and patient:

_____

_____

D. The opinion of a Non-Medical professional:

_____

_____

Q&A

What is the law if the patient says that the ailment is not lethal?

_____

_____

May the opinion of a gentile or non-religious doctor be trusted?

_____

_____

6. The law of Techum Shabbos by one who helped save another Jew

_____

_____

Shabbos Workbook

Additional Notes

Shabbos Workbook

May a doctor/ EMT which drove a patient to the hospital return home on Shabbos?

Chapter 2: The general rules for providing treatment to illnesses and ailments which are not deadly:

1. The law of one who has a limb that is in danger but is not life threatening

Q&A

What is the definition of the danger of a limb?

In cases that an action may only be done with an irregularity, what is defined to be an irregularity?

Is a Biblical action not done for its own use considered a Rabbinical action and allowed to be done by a Jew in cases that only a Rabbinical action is allowed to be done?

2. The law of one which is bedridden or feels weak in his entire body but is not in danger:

Q&A

In cases that an action may only be done with an irregularity, what is defined to be an irregularity?

Is a Biblical action not done for its own use considered a Rabbinical action and allowed to be done by a Jew in cases that only a Rabbinical action is allowed to be done?

May one who is bedridden or week in his entire body take medicine for a mere ache?

Shabbos Workbook

Additional Notes

Shabbos Workbook

Do the leniencies of a bedridden person apply even if he caused himself to reach this state, such as a failed suicide attempt?

In cases that an action may only be done with an irregularity, what is defined to be an irregularity?

Is a Biblical action not done for its own use considered a Rabbinical action and allowed to be done by a Jew in cases that only a Rabbinical action is allowed to be done?

---

4. One who is only slightly ill

---

5. One who has a mere ache

---

6. The status of a child with regards to desecrating Shabbos on their behalf and giving them medicine:

Q&A

Until what age are the typical needs of a child considered to be like the needs for one who is bedridden?

What needs of a child may be done as if he were bedridden?

May a child which is sick be given medicine even if he is not bedridden etc?

If a child needs food made for him to eat which involves a Shabbos transgression may it be done through a Jew?

Shabbos Workbook

Additional Notes

Shabbos Workbook

May one smear a cream onto a child's skin ones skin[?]

May one smear oil on a baby for healing purposes [such as he has a rash and the like]?

---

7. Taking Medicine and other medical treatments which involve no Shabbos prohibition:
A. The General Rule:

B. Taking medications and foods which are eaten for medication:

C. Giving medical treatment for symptoms which are never treated through medicine:

Q&A

May medicine be taken through an irregularity?

May one take aspirin and other pain reliever drugs on Shabbos?

May one take Vitamins?

May one insert a rectal suppository for medication?

May one take medication if he suspects that lack of doing so can lead to being bedridden or weak in his entire body?

346

Shabbos Workbook

<u>Additional Notes</u>

Shabbos Workbook

If one started a medication before Shabbos may he continue taking it into Shabbos?

Are medicines Muktzah?

May one open the closed covering of pills?

In a situation that one is allowed to take medicine may one mix a medicinal drink on Shabbos?

May a person who is in pain bathe in hot water heated before Shabbos?

May one place a wet cloth over his head to treat a fever or a head ache?

May one wear detachable braces on Shabbos?

May one wear a back brace and items of the sort?

May one take Sleeping pills:

May one take "stay awake pills"?

May one use nose drops?

Shabbos Workbook

<u>Additional Notes</u>

Shabbos Workbook

May one sniff or smell a substance that will clear his nasal passages?

May one smear a cream onto ones skin?

---

8. Giving assistance to a gentile which is giving the medical treatment:

---

9. May one ask a gentile to do an action which will only be needed for after Shabbos?

Chapter 3: List of Medical symptoms and their respective laws regarding their treatment:

1. Eye care:
A. Placing ointment in ones eye

B. Treatment for one who is unable to open his eyes:

C. Treating eye irritation

---

2. Mouth and Teeth ailments:
A. Removing the aching tooth:

B. Taking medicine

C. Chewing medicinal gum and applying toothpaste to ones teeth:

Shabbos Workbook

<u>Additional Notes</u>

Shabbos Workbook

Q&A

May one brush his teeth on Shabbos?

_____

_____

May one use mouthwash to remove bad odor:

_____

_____

3. A sore throat

_____

_____

May one drink a hot tea to sooth a sore throat?

_____

_____

4. Stomach care:
A. Inducing vomiting:

_____

_____

B. Treating stomach pains with a vessel of hot water

_____

_____

C. Dealing with constipation-Inducing Diarrhea:

_____

_____

Q&A

If the water is placed in a closed bottle may one place it on his stomach?

_____

_____

May one place an electric heating blanket [which was left on from before Shabbos] over an aching stomach?

_____

_____

May one take a laxative drug to help with constipation?

_____

_____

Shabbos Workbook

Additional Notes

Shabbos Workbook

May one insert a rectal suppository to treat constipation?

May one who has hemorrhoids apply ointment to the area?

May one who has hemorrhoids soak it in hot water?

5. Dislocated or broken arm or leg:
A. Dislocation:

B. Returning a broken bone to its proper positioning:

Q&A

If one is in great pain and there is fear that the limb will not be able to function properly any more if it is not returned to its socket may one be lenient to return it?

If one is in extreme pain but there is no fear of damaging the limb what is he to do?

May an x-ray be taken?

6. Skin care
A. Puncturing a pimple/boil on Shabbos

B. Scratching a pimple/boil on Shabbos

Shabbos Workbook

<u>Additional Notes</u>

Shabbos Workbook

C. Cutting off a blister

D. Removing a nail or pieces of skin from ones nail on Shabbos

Q&A

May one remove a nail which has peeled off in its majority?

May one apply Vaseline to dry lips on Shabbos?

May one apply powder or a spray to feet with bad odor?

May one cut or tear a bandage to make it a better fit?

May one use a piece of tape to tape the bandage onto ones skin?

May one cut a piece of tape to use?

May one tie the bandage onto his body, such as his arm or leg?

May one place a band-aid on a wound on Shabbos?

Shabbos Workbook

Additional Notes

Shabbos Workbook

May one remove a bandage that is taped onto his skin, such as a typical band-aid?

7. Treating wounds:

A. Cleaning the blood of a wound:

B. Squeezing out the blood

C. Applying ointments to a wound

D. Placing a substance on a wound which draws out puss and blood:

E. Applying ointment/liquids to suppress the bleeding of a wound

F. Placing sugar on a wound:

G. Widening the hole of a wound on Shabbos and the laws of an Apturah:

H. If cleaning a wound will cause blood to come out:

I. Placing pads and bandages on a wound on Shabbos:

Shabbos Workbook

Additional Notes

Shabbos Workbook

J. Applying oil or water to a bandage:

_____

_____

K. Placing a poultice [a bandage that contains ointment] on a wound

_____

_____

L. Switching the bandage of a wound

_____

_____

M. Removing scabs:

_____

_____

N. Removing splinters

_____

_____

Q&A

May a bandage be used over a bleeding wound?

_____

_____

May one wrap a towel over a bleeding wound?

_____

_____

May one wrap a tissue or napkin on the wound?

_____

_____

One who has cleaned a wound from blood, may he place on it a bandage even though he knows that it will eventually continue to bleed?

_____

_____

May one place Dermatol/Hydrogen Peroxide or other disinfecting liquids on a wound?

_____

_____

Shabbos Workbook

Additional Notes

Shabbos Workbook

May one smear a cream onto the wound?

8. Sobering up on Shabbos using different tactics:

9. Sobering up on Shabbos using different tactics

10. Sucking the milk from the breast of an animal to cure heart pain:

11. Pumping/squeezing milk from a woman in order to relive breast pain caused by the milk:

12. Exercising on Shabbos:

Q&A

May one do pushups, sit-ups, weight lifting and other forms of work outs?

May one do physiotherapy?

May one stretch his limbs?

May one do exercises on his hand?

Shabbos Workbook

Additional Notes

Shabbos Workbook

May one exercise his voice box through different breathing forms?

May one cause himself to sweat by covering himself with blankets?

May one take a suntan on Shabbos?

13. Massages:

14. Bathing for healing purposes:

List of illnesses and their status which are not mentioned in Shulchan Aruch:
1. One who has a standard fever [not lethal]:

2. One who has a headache?

3. One who has heartburn:

4. May one measure ones temperature to see if he is sick?

5. May one measure ones pulse to see if he is sick?

Shabbos Workbook

<u>**Additional Notes**</u>

Shabbos Workbook

6. May one get a shot on Shabbos?

_____

_____

Chapter 4: The law of Yoledes/Women during and after childbirth

1. Desecrating Shabbos on behalf of a Yoledes:

_____

_____

May one desecrate Shabbos on behalf of treating or preventing a miscarriage?

_____

_____

2. Preparing matters from before Shabbos

_____

_____

What matters are to be prepared from before Shabbos within the 9th month?

_____

_____

3. List of matters that may be done for a Yoledes:
A. Calling a midwife:

_____

_____

B. Desecrating Shabbos for non-essential matters which will calm her down:

_____

_____

Q&A

May a relative or friend accompany the Yoledes to the hospital?

_____

_____

May one travel to a hospital of their choice or must it be the closest available hospital?

_____

_____

May one who traveled to the hospital to give birth and was then released on Shabbos, due to being told that she is not ready to give birth, return home on Shabbos?

_____

_____

Shabbos Workbook

Additional Notes

Shabbos Workbook

4. From when does a woman carry the Halachic definition of a Yoledes:

_____

_____

Q&A

What is the practical definition today of sitting on the birthing stool?

_____

_____

What is the definition of blood coming out?

_____

_____

May one desecrate Shabbos if the woman's water broke?

_____

_____

If one has not yet reached the above stage but a Doctor says that Shabbos must be desecrated for her may one do so?

_____

_____

5. Matters which take time may be done before she reaches the Halachic state of a Yoledes:

_____

_____

6. Assisting a gentile women give birth:

_____

_____

Q&A

Practically today may one assist a gentile woman in giving birth, and may he desecrate Shabbos on her behalf?

_____

_____

7. Desecrating Shabbos for a woman which is after birth:
A. First three days after birth:

_____

_____

B. After 3 days but before 7 days after birth:

_____

_____

Shabbos Workbook

Additional Notes

Shabbos Workbook

C. From after seven days:

_____

_____

D. How to calculate the 7 days:

_____

_____

Q&A

If a woman had a miscarriage does she have the same status as a Yoledes in the above laws?

_____

_____

8. The law if a woman died r"l during childbirth:

_____

_____

9. What may be done for the new born on Shabbos?

_____

_____

Q&A

Practically, may one today desecrate Shabbos to help save a premature baby if it is in the eighth month?

_____

_____

May one desecrate Shabbos to help save a test tube baby [IVF]?

_____

_____

10. Pumping and squeezing milk on Shabbos:

_____

_____

Q&A

May a woman pump milk out to feed her baby if he refuses to suck from the breast?

_____

_____

May one squeeze the milk into the baby's mouth to stimulate it to eat?

_____

_____

Shabbos Workbook

Additional Notes

Shabbos Workbook

May a woman use a pump to release milk in order to relieve breast pain?

Chapter 5: Laws relating to a fire on Shabbos

1. The law if the fire poses a danger:

Q&A
Practically what is one to do if there is a small fire in one's home such as Shabbos candles?

2. Extinguishing a fire which merely poses a safety hazard:

3. Preventing a non-lethal fire from spreading:

Q&A
May one shake on to the floor a lit match or candle which has fallen onto one's tablecloth?

May one extinguish a spark?

4. Asking a gentile to extinguish a non-lethal fire:

5. A child who has come to extinguish the fire, must he be protested?

6. Extinguishing a metal coal:

Shabbos Workbook

Additional Notes

Shabbos Workbook

7. What may one save from a fire in one's home in a case that the fire does not pose a danger?
A. The general rules:

_____

_____

B. Saving food:

_____

_____

C. Saving clothing

_____

_____

D. Saving Sefarim

_____

_____

Q&A

May one save Lechem Mishneh for each meal?

_____

_____

May one save foods for desert?

_____

_____

How much liquid may one save?

_____

_____

May one remove a Mezuzah from a door to save it from a fire?

_____

_____

8. May one save his items from an approaching fire that is in his neighbor's home?

_____

_____

9. Saving items from robbers

_____

_____

Shabbos Workbook

10. Atonement for desecrating Shabbos for sake of saving belongings:

<u>Additional Notes</u>

Shabbos Workbook

The laws of Shabbos

Workbook

Volume 3

This Volume includes the Laws of:
Shearing
Writing and Erasing
Meameir
Sewing and Gluing
Reading
Music
Home Cleaning
Games
Plants and trees
Shabbos Bris
International Dateline

Compiled by Rabbi Yaakov Goldstein

Shabbos Workbook

The laws of Shearing: Removing hair, skin, and nails

1. The Av Melacha-Shearing wool from skin

2. Using one's hands to remove the wool

Q&A

May one pluck a feather from his piece of chicken?

3. Removing one's hair and nails
A. The General rules

B. May one ask a gentile to cut ones nails for Mikveh if they forgot to do so before Shabbos?

C. Removing a nail or pieces of skin from ones nail on Shabbos

Q&A

May one scrape dirt from under his nail?

May one scrape off part of the nail from under?

May one brush their hair on Shabbos?

378

Shabbos Workbook

Additional Notes

Shabbos Workbook

May one pluck hairs out from a garment made of animal skin?

Practically may one ask a gentile to cut the nails using a vessel or not?

What is the woman to do if a gentile is unable to remove the nails with her teeth or hands?

May one ask a gentile to remove also the toe nails?

May one remove a nail which has peeled off in its majority?

4. May one style their hair or undo the style on Shabbos?

Q&A

May one make a hair do on Shabbos?

May one use a soft brush to make the split?

May one use his hands to make the split?

May one use a comb to gather the hair and make it into a bow and the like?

Shabbos Workbook

Additional Notes

Shabbos Workbook

Do the above laws apply equally to a Sheitel?

_____

_____

Does the hair design prohibition apply to men as well?

_____

_____

May one twirl his Peiyos on Shabbos?

_____

_____

May one fold his beard on Shabbos?

_____

_____

5. May one brush their hair on Shabbos?

_____

_____

Q&A

May one softly brush their hair on Shabbos?

_____

_____

May one brush their Sheitel on Shabbos?

_____

_____

6. Cutting off a blister

_____

_____

7. Removing scabs

_____

_____

Q&A

May one remove a bandage that is taped onto his skin, such as a typical band-aid?

_____

_____

Shabbos Workbook

8. Removing lice from skins

<u>Additional Notes</u>

Shabbos Workbook

The Laws of Writing and Erasing on Shabbos:

Chapter 1: Writing letters, symbols, marks, pictures

1. The Av Melacha

_____

_____

2. The Biblical and Rabbinical Prohibitions

_____

_____

*2 Writing on condensation of fruits, windows, engraving in sand earth

_____

_____

Q&A

May one place toy letters next to each other thus forming a word?

_____

_____

May one place plastic letters onto a cake thus forming a word?

_____

_____

How long must the writing be able to last for it to be Biblically forbidden?

_____

_____

Is writing with a pencil Biblically forbidden?

_____

_____

Is writing on a black or marker board Biblically forbidden or only Rabbinically forbidden?

_____

_____

May one use a rubber stamp on Shabbos?

_____

_____

Shabbos Workbook

Additional Notes

Shabbos Workbook

Is typing on a computer considered writing?

_____

_____

May one write on carbon paper?

_____

_____

3. Drawings and designs

_____

_____

Q&A

May one put together puzzles on Shabbos?

_____

_____

May one engrave designs onto his food or cake?

_____

_____

Does taking a picture with a camera, scanner, x-ray involve the writing prohibition?

_____

_____

4. Figuratively writing in the air or on a table and the like:

_____

_____

Q&A

May one write using a magnetic board?

_____

_____

May one use a thermometer strap which reveals letters or numbers upon being heated?

_____

_____

May one take a pregnancy test on Shabbos?

_____

_____

Shabbos Workbook

Additional Notes

Shabbos Workbook

May one make letters and words using sticks or threads?

_____

_____

May one form letters and pictures using his fingers [meaning by placing them in positions that form an item or symbol]?

_____

_____

5. Engraving letters [or pictures]:
A. Onto leather

_____

_____

B. On to earth, sand, fat, honey, water:

_____

_____

6. Making marks on books/parchment and the like:
A. On leather and parchment:

_____

_____

B. Making a mark on Paper:

_____

_____

C. Writing symbols

_____

_____

D. Making lines on skin and paper

_____

_____

Q&A

May one write numbers?

_____

_____

May one take a fingerprint on Shabbos?

_____

_____

Shabbos Workbook

<u>Additional Notes</u>

Shabbos Workbook

May one bend a page in a book as a reminder?

_____

_____

7. Entering letters into clothing

_____

_____

May one enter letters into a necklace or bracelet?

_____

_____

8. Closing and opening books with writing [or designs] on their side pages

_____

_____

Q&A

If the page of a book is torn may one place the page together in order to read it?

_____

_____

May one open or close curtains or doors which form words, letters or pictures upon opening or closing them?

_____

_____

General Q&A

May one use a combination lock on Shabbos?

_____

_____

May one put together puzzles on Shabbos?

_____

_____

May one play scrabble?

_____

_____

May one engrave designs onto his food or cake?

_____

_____

Shabbos Workbook

<u>Additional Notes</u>

Shabbos Workbook

Chapter 2: Erasing:

1. The Biblical Prohibition

_____

_____

May one separate letters from a word if the letters will remain intact?

_____

_____

2. To erase without intent to write:

_____

_____

3. To erase drawings and designs

_____

_____

4. Erasing ink/dye splotches and removing wax in order to write:

_____

_____

Q&A

May one erase ink splotches without intent to write in its place?

_____

_____

May one remove a fresh ink splotch which is not yet dry?

_____

_____

May one remove food splotches or other splotches from a book, such as a bentcher?

_____

_____

May one remove ink or dye blotches from ones table or other non-writing surfaces?

_____

_____

May one wash ink blotches or letters and drawings off his skin?

_____

_____

Shabbos Workbook

Additional Notes

Shabbos Workbook

May one wash his hands for bread or prayer if they have ink blotches, letters or drawings on them?

_____

_____

May one wash his hands from soot that got on them, as is common when moving pots?

_____

_____

May one remove glue from one's skin on Shabbos?

_____

_____

5. Removing wax [and the like] from letters to see the letters more clearly:

_____

_____

Q&A

May one remove food splotches or other splotches from letters in order to see the letters better?

_____

_____

May one remove wax blotches [as well as other forms of blotches] from letters of a Sefer Torah and does it invalidate the Torah?

_____

_____

6. One who edits letters:

_____

_____

7. Eating cake with letterings:

_____

_____

8. Closing and opening books with writing on their side pages:

_____

_____

Practical Q&A

May one wash ink blotches or letters and drawings off his skin?

_____

_____

Shabbos Workbook

May one open a cap of a bottle and the like which has engraved letters which will be broken upon opening it?

May one break an egg on Shabbos by the pink letters area?

May one cut Chalah together with its label on Shabbos?

May one tear the wrapper of a food that contains words or pictures on it?

May one use tissues or toilet paper that has letters or pictures on them?

May one erase letters or pictures on a magnetic board?

<u>Additional Notes</u>

Shabbos Workbook

The laws of Meameir- Gathering Scattered items on Shabbos:

1. The Av Melacha

_____

_____

2. The Biblical Prohibition:
A. The Gathering is being done in area of growth unless being pressed into one mass

_____

_____

B. Items that grow from the ground:

_____

_____

3. The Rabbinical prohibition-Gathering items that do not grow from ground in their area of growth:

_____

_____

4. Permitted form of gathering-Gathering from out of area of growth:

_____

_____

5. Gathering scattered fruits:
A. From under the tree which they grew on

_____

_____

B. From an area which they have not grown in

_____

_____

Q&A

May one gather the fruit into his pocket or shirt in a case that it may not be gathered into a basket?

_____

_____

If the fruits are in danger of being ruined if left un-gathered may one be lenient to gather them into a basket?

_____

_____

Shabbos Workbook

<u>Additional Notes</u>

Shabbos Workbook

Does the above restriction to only gather items a little at a time in order to use and not place in a basket apply by all scattered items or only by fruit?

_____

_____

Does this restriction against placing a selected food into a basket apply to other foods as well or only to fruits that have fallen into earth?

_____

_____

May one gather eggs from a chicken coop on Shabbos?

_____

_____

May one gather non-Muktzah papers which have scattered on the floor?

_____

_____

May one gather apples which fell and scattered on ones floor?

_____

_____

May one make a necklace or bracelet by entering items into them?

_____

_____

Shabbos Workbook

Additional Notes

Shabbos Workbook

The Laws of Sewing, Gluing and Taping items Together on Shabbos:

1. The Biblical prohibition-Sewing a stable set of stitches

_____

_____

Q&A

May one attach two sides of his clothing using a safety pin?

_____

May one staple papers together or remove staples from papers on Shabbos?

_____

May one attach an item to a bulletin board using push pins?

_____

May one place a clasp on an ace bandage to fasten it together?

_____

May one enter or remove papers from a metal binder on Shabbos?

_____

Is zippering two items together forbidden due to the sewing prohibition?

_____

May one zipper the wool lining on to a coat?

_____

May one attach items together using Velcro?

_____

May magnets be used on Shabbos to attach items to a metal surface?

_____

_____

Shabbos Workbook

<u>Additional Notes</u>

Shabbos Workbook

2. The Rabbinical prohibition-sewing an unstable set of stitches

3. Pulling a thread to tighten the connection between the parts of clothing

Q&A

May one pull the drawstring of a garbage bag or sweat pants to tighten it?

May one tighten a loose button through pulling on one of its threads?

4. Weaving and unraveling ropes and wicks

5. Gluing things together

Q&A

May one use scotch tape on Shabbos to tape things together?

May one use a piece of tape to tape a bandage onto ones skin?

May one place pictures into an album which contains cellophane to keep the picture in place?

May one use "post it" notes on Shabbos?

Shabbos Workbook

May one seal an envelope on Shabbos?

May one reattach the tape of a Sefer which is beginning to peel off?

6. The Tearing prohibition- Tearing sewed items and separating items that were glued together?

Q&A

May one separate items that were intentionally glued for temporary purpose?

May one place a band-aid on a wound on Shabbos?

May one use diapers on Shabbos which are fastened using a piece of tape or Velcro?

<u>Additional Notes</u>

Shabbos Workbook

<u>Reading on Shabbos- The laws pertaining to reading books, papers, documents and other forms of writing:</u>

1. Reading business documents and contracts:

_____

_____

2. Reading non-business related writings:

_____

_____

3. Reading the guest list for one's meal:

_____

_____

4. Reading engraved writings:

_____

_____

5. Reading Mitzvah related matters:

_____

_____

Q&A

May one read words written on the Peroches; Bimah etc?

_____

_____

May one read the names of the deceased when no charity is being given in connection with it?

_____

_____

6. Reading to the public matters which pertain to the community

_____

_____

7. Reading mail:
A. The law regarding when it is permitted to be read:

_____

_____

Shabbos Workbook

<u>Additional Notes</u>

Shabbos Workbook

B. Are forbidden letters Muktzah?

C. Not to take the mail from the postman's hand

Q&A

May one open up an envelope to remove its letter?

8. Reading descriptions written under designs, portraits and paintings

9. Reading books:
A. History books and novels:

B. Books of wisdoms, such as Medical books and the like:

Q&A

May one read a book on Shabbos for the purpose of editing it after Shabbos?

May one read from the manuscript of a Sefer which is meant for editing?

May one read a Torah book on Shabbos for the purpose of writing about it after Shabbos, as is common with Chidushei Torah, or homework of Limudei Kodesh?

May one read a non-Torah book on Shabbos for the purpose of writing about it after Shabbos?

Shabbos Workbook

<u>Additional Notes</u>

Shabbos Workbook

May one prepare the Torah reading on Shabbos for the sake of the next week's portion?

May one make a marking on a book in order to remember a place that needs correction, or the page that he is on?

10. Are writings which are forbidden to be read on Shabbos Muktzah?

Q&A

May one read a newspaper?

May one read a cook book?

May one read announcements placed on a bulletin board?

May a list which one wrote before Shabbos be read on Shabbos?

Shabbos Workbook

Additional Notes

Shabbos Workbook

The laws of Music; Noisemaking, Clapping and Dancing on Shabbos

1. Making sounds, rhythms or music on Shabbos using an instrument or vessel:

_____

_____

Q&A

May one ring bells or other instruments with an irregularity?

_____

May a child play with toys that make music or noise?

_____

May one make noise with a baby toy in order to lull a baby to sleep?

_____

May one move a Torah crown with bells on Shabbos?

_____

May one dress children in clothing that have bells?

_____

May one knock on the door with his key?

_____

May one who is bedridden ring for a nurse using a mechanical bell?

_____

May one drum on one's table?

_____

2. Are instruments which are designated to make music or noise Muktzah on Shabbos?

_____

_____

Shabbos Workbook

<u>Additional Notes</u>

Shabbos Workbook

Q&A

Examples of Musical items and their Muktzah status:

_____

_____

Are toys which are not designated specifically for noise or music making, but do so in the process of being used, considered Muktzah?

_____

_____

3. Clapping, dancing and snapping one's finger on Shabbos:

_____

_____

Q&A

May one whistle through placing his fingers in his mouth?

_____

_____

May one snap his fingers in order to wake someone up or get their attention?

_____

_____

May one clap in order to wake someone up or to get their attention?

_____

_____

May one clap after a speech?

_____

_____

Dancing and clapping on Simchas Torah:

_____

_____

May one ring bells on Simchas Torah?

_____

_____

May one dance and clap for a Mitzvah purpose?

_____

_____

Shabbos Workbook

May one dance and clap to a Niggun on Shabbos and Yom Tov?

_____

_____

May one drum his hands or a vessel on the table in beat of a song or Niggun?

_____

_____

4. Making noise to chase away animals and birds:

_____

_____

<u>Additional Notes</u>

Shabbos Workbook

Home cleanliness- The laws involved in cleaning and repairing one's home on Shabbos

Sweeping and Mopping [Halachas 1-4]

1. Sweeping on Shabbos:

_____

_____

Q&A

May one sweep a carpet?

_____

_____

List of brooms and their law:

_____

_____

May one screw in the rod of a broom into a broom?

_____

_____

2. Is a broom Muktzah?

_____

_____

3. May one brush his clothing using a brush or broom?

_____

_____

Q&A

May one clean furniture?

_____

_____

4. Mopping on Shabbos:

_____

_____

Q&A

If liquid spilled on one's floor may one squeegee the water?

_____

_____

Shabbos Workbook

<u>Additional Notes</u>

Shabbos Workbook

May one remove the drain cover of one's floor on Shabbos in order to squeegee spilled water into the hole?

_____

_____

If water spilled on one's floor may one place a rag over the water to clean it up?

_____

_____

May one clean with water a dirty spot on the ground?

_____

_____

May one wash and dry one's counter?

_____

_____

May one ask a gentile to mop his floor?

_____

_____

May one polish his floor on Shabbos?

_____

_____

May a hospital mop the floors for hygienic purposes?

_____

_____

Moving Furniture
5. Dragging furniture across one's floor or ground:

_____

_____

Q&A

May one push a baby carriage over an earth floor, such as over the ground outside, in a place where there is an Eiruv?

_____

_____

May one push a wheel chair over an earth floor?

_____

_____

Shabbos Workbook

Additional Notes

Shabbos Workbook

Are closets and book cases which are designated to a specific area allowed to be moved?

_____

_____

Cleaning one's table
6. The laws of removing leftovers from ones table:

_____

_____

Q&A

May one initially place bread on the table in order to be allowed to remove the tablecloth, or must the bread be there before the inedible foods were placed on the table?

_____

_____

Do items other than bread which are placed on the table also allow one to move the tablecloth?

_____

_____

Cleaning spills
7. How to clean spills on Shabbos:

_____

_____

Q&A

May one clean a spill using napkins or tissues?

_____

_____

May one clean a dry table/counter using a wet cloth?

_____

_____

May one rub dry a wet counter or table [that does not contain an absorbent table cloth] using a dry cloth?

_____

_____

May one wipe the liquid off a wet tablecloth using a knife and the like?

_____

_____

Shabbos Workbook

Additional Notes

Shabbos Workbook

May one move a wet rag or napkin that was used to clean a spill?

_____

_____

May one use baby wipes on Shabbos to clean a table and the like?

_____

_____

Garbage
8. Removing the garbage:

_____

_____

Cleaning dishes
9. Washing dishes on Shabbos:

_____

_____

Q&A on washing Dishes
May one wash dirty dishes even if he has clean dishes available?

_____

_____

May one wash the dishes after his last meal if they are tarnishing the cleanliness of the house?

_____

_____

May one wash dishes on Shabbos if he will only be using them the next Shabbos?

_____

_____

May one soak the dishes in water after his last Shabbos meal?

_____

_____

May one wash his food pots on Shabbos?

_____

_____

May one enter water into his food pot in order to let the pot soak?

_____

_____

Shabbos Workbook

<u>Additional Notes</u>

Shabbos Workbook

May one wash his Kiddush cup out after Kiddush of the day meal?

_____

_____

Which soaps may be used to wash dishes?

_____

_____

May one place soap into a cup of liquid and have it dissolve and then use that to wash dishes?

_____

_____

Which forms of sponges may be used to wash the dishes?

_____

_____

10. Scrubbing, Shining and Polishing dishes and silverware:

_____

_____

Q&A on Polishing

May one polish glass dishes?

_____

_____

May one polish silverware, copperware and other silver vessels?

_____

_____

May one remove rust from metal, such as from the blade of a knife?

_____

_____

Tevilas Keilim
11. Immersing vessels in a Mikveh:

_____

_____

Q&A

May one immerse a vessel on Shabbos if there is a doubt as to whether it requires immersion?

_____

_____

Shabbos Workbook

<u>Additional Notes</u>

Shabbos Workbook

12. May one unplug a drain pipe on Shabbos?

_____

_____

Q&A

May one unplug a stuffed toilet or sink?

_____

_____

13. May one undo a storage room of non-Muktzah items?

_____

_____

14. Undoing the storage for the sake of a Mitzvah?

_____

_____

15. How to undo the storage room, when needed for the sake of a Mitzvah:

_____

_____

General Q&A

If a Mezuzah fell off the doorpost may one reattach it?

_____

_____

May one remove cobwebs on Shabbos?

_____

_____

May one spray air freshener in his room or bathroom?

_____

_____

May one use a toilet that contains toilet soap?

_____

_____

May one clean a dirty toilet?

_____

_____

Shabbos Workbook

<u>Additional Notes</u>

Shabbos Workbook

<u>Playing Games on Shabbos:</u>

1. Playing games on Shabbos:

_____

_____

2. Doing a lottery on Shabbos:

_____

_____

3. May one play ball on Shabbos?

_____

_____

4. Running and jumping games:

_____

_____

5. Reading Books:

_____

_____

General Q&A

May an adult play games on Shabbos?

_____

Are games which adults may not play considered Muktzah?

_____

May one play with play dough on Shabbos?

_____

May one play ball on Shabbos?

_____

May one play ping pong on Shabbos?

_____

_____

Shabbos Workbook

Additional Notes

Shabbos Workbook

May one inflate a balloon?

May a child play building games such as Lego and the like?

May one form a ship, plane and the like from [non-Muktzah] paper?

May one blow bubbles on Shabbos?

Is snow Muktzah?

May one make snow balls and snow men?

May one ride a bicycle on Shabbos?

May one ride roller blades?

May one play in a sand box on Shabbos?

May one put together puzzles on Shabbos?

May one play chess?

Shabbos Workbook

Additional Notes

Shabbos Workbook

May one play scrabble?

_____

_____

May one play Monopoly?

_____

_____

May one play dreidal?

_____

_____

May a child play with toys that make music or noise?

_____

_____

May one use a swing which is attached to a tree?

_____

_____

May one watch a game on a neighbor's television or go see a game in a stadium?

_____

_____

Shabbos Workbook

Additional Notes

Shabbos Workbook

Laws relating to plants, trees, and garden produce:

1. Making use of trees on Shabbos:
A. Climbing:

B. Hanging on a tree:

C. Leaning on a tree:

D. Touching a tree:

E. Making use of a tree for one's objects:

F. May one place an item on a tree before Shabbos having it remain there into Shabbos?

G. Making use of items which are attached to a tree:

H. Making use of tree roots:

I. Making use of branches of a tree:

J. Making use of the trunk of a tree:

Shabbos Workbook

<u>Additional Notes</u>

Shabbos Workbook

Q&A

If one's Tallis got stuck on a tree may one remove it?

May one lie on a hammock which is attached to a tree?

May one use a swing which is attached to a tree?

May one climb into a tree house on Shabbos?

May one make use of a tree which grows in a pod?

2. Making use of plants and grass on Shabbos:

3. Walking on Grass:

Q&A

May one walk quickly on blades of grass?

May one walk on stalks which break upon walking over them?

If blades of grass, thorns and the like became stuck in one's shoes may one remove it?

Shabbos Workbook

Additional Notes

Shabbos Workbook

4. Smelling fruits, flowers and plants that are still attached to the ground:

_____

_____

5. Scenting branches and leaves that are detached from the ground:

_____

_____

Q&A

May one smell scented leaves of a pod plant?

_____

_____

6. Fruits which fell off a tree:

_____

_____

Q&A

Are vegetables which detached from the ground on Shabbos forbidden to be eaten?

_____

_____

7. Watering plants and grass:

_____

_____

Q&A

May one pour water over plain earth?

_____

_____

May one pour water over plain earth if it is near grass or plants?

_____

_____

May one eat over bare earth that has no grass or plants?

_____

_____

May one urinate over earth?

_____

_____

Shabbos Workbook

Additional Notes

Shabbos Workbook

May one urinate onto mud?

_____

_____

May one wash in a sink which has a drainage pipe that draws the water onto plants or seeded soil?

_____

_____

May one spit onto plants, or grass?

_____

_____

\May one spit onto plain earth?

_____

_____

May one pour a plant killing agent over plants on Shabbos?

_____

_____

May one water a pod plant that does not have any breathing holes?

_____

_____

May one cover plants which are outside to protect them from rain?

_____

_____

If rain water has gathered over ones awning or Schach covering, may it be removed if it will subsequently cause the water to fall onto grass and the like?

_____

_____

8. Uprooting plants and other growths from their source:
A. The general rule:

_____

_____

B. Case examples:

_____

_____

Shabbos Workbook

<u>Additional Notes</u>

Shabbos Workbook

C. Laws relating to Pod Plants:

_____

_____

D. Removing garden produce that is insulated within earth:

_____

_____

E. Picking fruits from a branch which has fallen:

_____

_____

Q&A

How large does the hole of a pod have to be for it to be considered a breathing hole?

_____

_____

What is the status if the pod only has a hole on its side and not its bottom?

_____

_____

May one move a pod plant within one's house?

_____

_____

Is a pod considered Muktzah and thus even when allowed to be moved, it is only to be moved in ways permitted by Muktzah?

_____

_____

May one move a tree which grows in a pod in one's house?

_____

_____

May one move a pod plant from on the earth or on a peg into one's home or vice versa?

_____

_____

May one move a pod plant from one area of the earth to another?

_____

_____

Shabbos Workbook

Additional Notes

Shabbos Workbook

May one move a pod that is sitting on a tray together with its tray?

May one open the window to allow the plants to breath fresh air, or for rain to fall on them?

May one close the window to prevent the cold air from damaging the plants?

May one cover plants to protect them from the cold?

May one move the plants towards the sun in order for them to further grow?

May one remove dates from its stalk?

May one remove bananas, grapes and other fruits from their vine?

---

9. Throwing seeds and pits onto the ground:

---

10. Placing kernels in water on Shabbos:

Q&A

May one remove kernels that have begun to grow from within their water?

Shabbos Workbook

Additional Notes

Shabbos Workbook

May one remove an avocado pit from water if it has begun to sprout?

_____

_____

May one plant seeds in the ground with intent to remove them prior to them growing?

_____

_____

11. Placing flowers and plants into water on Shabbos:

_____

_____

Q&A

May one sprinkle water onto detached flowers and plants?

_____

_____

May one move the flowers towards the sun in order that they open?

_____

_____

May one remove plants from the water on Shabbos?

_____

_____

May one make a flower bouquet on Shabbos?

_____

_____

12. Watering detached vegetables:

_____

_____

Shabbos Workbook

Additional Notes

Shabbos Workbook

The Laws involved in performing a Bris on Shabbos:

1. In what scenarios is a child to be circumcised on Shabbos?

_____

_____

Q&A

May one circumcise the child of an unorthodox couple on Shabbos if doing so will lead to unnecessary desecration of Shabbos?

_____

_____

Must a Mohel agree to travel away from home to do a Shabbos Milah?

_____

_____

One who follows Rabbeinu Tam regarding Motzaei Shabbos, how is he to follow regarding a child born after sunset?

_____

_____

If a child was born on Shabbos with use of a vacuum is he to be circumcised on his 8th day which coincides with Shabbos?

_____

_____

Is an IVF or AI baby to be circumcised on his 8th day which coincides with Shabbos?

_____

_____

2. Actions that may be performed for the child when a Bris is performed on Shabbos:

_____

_____

3. Machshireiy Milah/Transgressions involved in preparing for the circumcision:

_____

_____

4. Bathing the infant:

_____

_____

Shabbos Workbook

<u>Additional Notes</u>

Shabbos Workbook

5. Washing the baby with a wet cloth:

_____

_____

6. Is a Mila knife Muktzah on a Shabbos Bris?

_____

_____

Q&A

Is the foreskin Muktzah?

_____

_____

7. May one perform his first Bris on Shabbos?

_____

_____

8. Having two people do the Milah and Periah:

_____

_____

Shabbos Workbook

Additional Notes

Shabbos Workbook

Laws which relate to the Date of Shabbos, International Dateline, and Time zones

1. One who is lost in the desert or wilderness and has lost track of days, when does he keep Shabbos?

_____

_____

Q&A

If one has been captured and no longer has track of which day is Shabbos what is he to do?

_____

_____

Is one to wear Tefillin on his seventh day?

_____

_____

If one of the days is for certain a weekday, as explained above, then if he is able to work enough on this day to supply food for all the other days must he do so?

_____

_____

Q&A relating to changes in time zones

When does one keep Shabbos in Japan and New Zealand?

_____

_____

In areas which the daylight or night lasts for more than 24 hours, how is Shabbos calculated?

_____

_____

May one who owns a business in a later time zone have the business open at the conclusion of Shabbos of his time zone?

_____

_____

In the above scenario may the business remain open on Erev Shabbos until Shabbos begins in its time zone, or must it close at the time the owner accepts Shabbos?

_____

_____

May one call or send a fax to an area of a later time zone if Shabbos has not yet ended there?

_____

_____

Shabbos Workbook

<u>Additional Notes</u>

Shabbos Workbook

May one send an e-mail to a person of a later time zone if Shabbos has not yet ended there?

_____

_____

May one travel after Shabbos to a country that is in a later time zone?

_____

_____

Printed in Great Britain
by Amazon